Marcia Williams

MARCIA WILLIAMS

The Life and Times of Baroness Falkender

Linda McDougall

Biteback Publishing

First published in Great Britain in 2023 by
Biteback Publishing Ltd, London
Copyright © Linda McDougall 2023

Linda McDougall has asserted her right under the Copyright, Designs and Patents Act 1988
to be identified as the author of this work.

Extracts from Marcia Field's articles in *The Cub* student newspaper reproduced by kind
permission of Queen Mary, University of London Archives: Queen Mary College;
QMC/CUB/2; CUB, 14 May 1954.

Extracts from Thames Television's 1984 interview with Marcia Falkender by Judith Chalmers
reproduced by kind permission of FremantleMedia UK.

Every reasonable effort has been made to trace copyright holders of material reproduced in this
book, but if any have been inadvertently overlooked the publisher would be glad to hear from them.

ISBN 978-1-78590-752-4

10 9 8 7 6 5 4 3 2 1

A CIP catalogue record for this book is available from the British Library.

Set in Minion Pro and Bodoni

Printed and bound in Great Britain by
CPI Group (UK) Ltd, Croydon CR0 4YY

FSC
www.fsc.org
MIX
Paper | Supporting
responsible forestry
FSC® C171272

In memory of Austin Mitchell

Contents

Introduction

An Influential and Divisive Figure

Whether or not you approved of Margaret Thatcher, there can be little doubt that she was the most significant female British politician of the twentieth century. Who, though, came second?

This book sets out the case for awarding the silver medal to Marcia Williams, ennobled in 1974 as Baroness Falkender. She was best known officially as the private and political secretary to Harold Wilson, Prime Minister of Great Britain between 1964 and 1970 and again from 1974 to 1976, and unofficially as the first woman to run the country from 10 Downing Street, over a decade before Thatcher took office.

I have been a political 'insider' and observer of British politics since the 1960s. My late husband, Austin Mitchell, was the Labour MP for Grimsby between 1977 and his retirement in 2015, and I have been a television documentary maker and journalist for over forty years, working on projects such as *World in Action*'s 'Why I Want to Be Leader by Margaret Thatcher' and *Westminster Women*, published by Vintage in 1998, right through to the Channel 4 Political Awards that ran for a decade but died overnight in the wake of the

MPs' expenses scandal. In all that time, I saw a hell of a lot of politicians, but I never met Marcia. She was much more of an insider than me.

Austin was one of those who did know her, and it was our discussions about her and how society and politics had moved on since her reign in No. 10 which motivated me to write this book. It turned out we had a lot in common, Marcia and I, from our passion for Yorkshire politicians to our eagerness for the advancement of equality for women.

In their own way, both Marcia and Austin were Labour Party mavericks who stood outside the party's mainstream. He was a long-serving backbench MP who never achieved ministerial office. He was never a team player, stubborn and individualistic but kind and popular on both sides of the house yet cursed like so many by bad luck in timing – he became an MP after winning a by-election just two years before the 1979 general election. He was sixty-three when Tony Blair came to power in 1997 – a generation older than the 44-year-old New Labour leader.

Marcia Williams, on the other hand, never stood for or sought public office. She talent-spotted Harold Wilson in 1956, when she was a 24-year-old secretary working in Transport House, the Labour Party's head office, and remained by his side, an increasingly influential and divisive figure, for the next forty years.

Although Marcia lived until 2019, she was out of the public eye long before Harold Wilson died in 1995 and is largely forgotten now. In her heyday and afterwards, her critics wondered why Wilson was so loyal to her. They regretted, privately and in public, what they regard as her baleful influence on him. While recognising and discussing her faults and her failings, I try to offer a more balanced view of her achievements. Like so much of life, it should never have been a binary choice – you didn't have to be either for Marcia or against her. But for too many, it was. And the loudest voices were against. This book seeks to rescue Marcia – a simply brilliant tactician and politician – from the patronising, misogynistic and dismissive verdicts of various male enemies and to suggest a more nuanced context to and understanding of her actions and reactions.

In my view, there is a strong argument that Harold Wilson's political successes were a direct result of his recognition and acceptance that he needed the support that Marcia's practical and organisational skills and active and acute political antennae offered. It was a genuine and enduring partnership between a man and a woman at the top of the political ladder, never seen before or since in British politics.

In modern parlance, Marcia had Harold's back, unconditionally, for decades, during which many of his colleagues saw it as a target for their daggers. The price he inevitably paid, though, was a whispering campaign echoing down the years that she must have had 'something' on Harold for him to put up with her for so long. Because she was, particularly in later years, prone to acting like a prima donna and causing trouble when working as political secretary to a Prime Minister sixteen years her senior, tales about her abounded.

Westminster has long been notorious as a gossip-infected bubble. Sometimes the gossip is true; often not – or it has been exaggerated or inflated by those with an agenda. Marcia was a victim of this relentless rumour mill. She was lucky she was politically active before the internet age, when it would have been so much worse for her. Some stories appear in this book that have been hard to either prove or disprove but seemed to me to warrant inclusion in order to present as rounded a view as possible of her vital contributions to public and political life in the 1960s and '70s.

Many of the people who gave Marcia a helping hand are now dead. Others, embarrassed by the possibility of a vicious backlash, stay silent.

As a result, there are gaps in the narrative, especially after Harold Wilson's retirement through the gradual decline in Marcia's health until her eventual death in the Newstead Lodge Nursing Home in Southam in Warwickshire in 2019. The Bodleian Library's Wilson collection has desk diaries from 1975 until Harold's death in 1995. Meticulously but sparsely filled in by Marcia, they record trips to the doctor and dentist, the Scilly Isles and an annual visit to Bob and Betty Maxwell's home in Oxford. The sad vapour trail after a hectic political life.

Although both Harold Wilson and Marcia Williams wrote conventional memoirs, they are less than illuminating when it comes to the details of their complex and lengthy relationship. Others have filled some of the gaps and I have quoted from their works or summarised their views where I felt it appropriate to do so and where they could add value to the story.

Since this is not an 'academic' book, more a personal attempt to understand what made Marcia tick and prove how and why she should be recognised as a groundbreaking female Labour Party pioneer, I have not provided footnotes. I hope the story of Marcia will attract readers who would run a mile to avoid a conventional political biography but enjoy the story of her outstanding contribution to British political history and her stunning disregard for the rules of the game as dictated by some of the men who ran Britain in the 1960s and '70s.

When Harold Wilson made the shock announcement of his retirement as Prime Minister in 1976, Marcia was immediately outed as the creator of the 'Lavender List' – Wilson's suggestions for honours for those who had served Britain and the Labour government. The list, in Marcia's handwriting on lilac notepaper, had apparently been dictated by Harold as he dashed along a corridor in No. 10 and jotted down by Marcia running beside him, pen and paper at the ready. Well, that was what Harold and Marcia claimed, but Joe Haines (Wilson's press secretary) and a great many journalists, civil servants and politicians believed the Lavender List was dreamed up by Marcia alone, to reward people who had helped her out financially and perhaps even sexually while she had been working with the Prime Minister. The story and angry discussions about who to blame lived on well into the twenty-first century when the BBC commissioned a drama, *The Lavender List*, written by Francis Wheen, the deputy editor of *Private Eye*, and based on Joe Haines's memoirs and Bernard Donoughue's diaries. As soon as it was broadcast, Marcia sued the BBC and settled out of court for £70,000 and the promise that the BBC would never show the drama again. To this day, the story of the Lavender List has cast a long shadow over Wilson's legacy and cost Marcia her place in history.

The past for women is often a blurry negative of cooking, pot washing, childbirth and a few clever grannies who could crack codes at Bletchley Park or protested against cruise missiles at Greenham Common. It's so important that we begin telling more women's stories – the good, the bad and the mundane. We have a right to our history, to find out how tough it was for the women who went before, and a right to be proud of them for their achievements, no matter how big or small.

This book is the story of one woman, daughter, mother, aunt and grandmother just eight years older than me who was a pioneer in twentieth-century Britain. The first woman to wield real power in 10 Downing Street, Marcia has, however, been forgotten by the historical narrative. It's time to restore her to her rightful place among the great and the good of the Labour Party and British political history.

1

Who Was Marcia?

When Queen Elizabeth II acceded to the throne on 6 February 1952, there were just eighteen female MPs in a House of Commons of 650 members. When Charles III became king seventy years later, over a third of the whole House were women. For the first time there were more female Labour MPs than male, and just over a third of all the Conservative government ministers were women.

The seventy years of Elizabeth's reign neatly encompass the adult working life of Baroness Marcia Falkender, the first woman of real power at the top of a British government. Marcia was political secretary, political partner and adviser to Harold Wilson, who was Labour Prime Minister from 1964–70 and 1974–76. She masterminded his victory as leader of the Labour Party after the death of Hugh Gaitskell, and she was a strong and expert adviser at his side when he triumphed in four general elections. Most important of all, Harold Wilson and Marcia Falkender were an unbreakable partnership, politically wedded to each other and equal contributors to his first general election victory on 15 October 1964. From that moment on, however, her power and her position were constantly challenged. Misogyny, jealousy, a private life that shocked those who knew about it and accusations of money-grubbing and bribery all contributed to her reputation as a public nuisance who needed to be got rid of. Urgently.

The world has changed utterly since 1956 when Marcia Williams, an ambitious and politically astute young graduate from London Queen Mary College, got a job working with Harold Wilson, an equally ambitious Member of Parliament sixteen years her senior. Yorkshireman Harold was a scholarship boy, Oxford educated and regarded as 'brilliant' by the academics who taught him, the civil servants he worked with and his Labour Party colleagues.

Northampton scholarship girl Marcia, daughter of generations of bricklayers and builders and a mother who believed that she herself was the illegitimate daughter of King Edward VII, had some of that all-important 'extra value' necessary for a woman making her way to the top in the 1950s: a qualification in shorthand and typing from St Godric's Secretarial College in Hampstead.

In Paul Gallico's 1958 story *Mrs Harris Goes to Paris*, filmed again in 2022, Mrs Harris, a London cleaner with a passion for haute couture, cheerfully explains to Christian Dior and his executives facing strikes and bankruptcy that if they sack most of their female staff they will be bankrupt even quicker. Mrs Harris summed up perfectly the contribution made by the female workers to the famous fashion house: 'We clean up everybody's mess and make everything in the garden lovely. We're the ones they rely on. They don't even know what we do, but without us, it all goes tits-up!'

It was just the same in politics. Many female Labour Party members spent the whole of their membership in the kitchen at their local Labour HQ, very occasionally wiping their hands on their aprons and appearing at the back of the room when an election had been won, or an MP retired. Marcia was different.

One person who knew her in the late '50s, the future BBC political editor John Cole, recalls spotting Marcia's political abilities as soon as they met:

I had known Marcia Williams from shortly after my arrival in London when she was Harold's secretary and he was shadow Chancellor. She had a sharp political brain and after he became Prime Minister, she was often helpful to me in giving a well-balanced judgement of how the Labour Party would react to some policy. Although nominally an adviser, she was amongst the shrewdest Labour politicians of her period.

John Cole also praised Marcia's skill when it came to winning elections:

Just before the 1964 election campaign she was leafing through the *Radio Times* to check if anything appearing on television on the eve of polling day might reduce the turnout of voters. To her horror she discovered that *Steptoe and Son*, one of the most popular programmes of the period which at its peak could draw 28 million viewers, was scheduled an hour before the polls closed, the time when the largest number of Labour supporters traditionally came out to vote.

Marcia informed Harold, who called the BBC director-general Hugh Carleton Greene, to argue that this temptation could reduce the turnout of Conservative as well as Labour voters. Sir Hugh dryly asked the Leader of the Opposition to suggest an appropriate alternative programme.

'Greek drama, preferably in the original,' joked Harold.

The BBC agreed to move *Steptoe*. Labour won 317 seats, the Conservatives 304 and the Liberals nine, an overall majority of just four seats. Later Wilson said that but for Marcia and her ingenuity, he would never have become Prime Minister.

Today, like so many women of the past, key workers and influential in so many fields, Marcia Williams is almost entirely forgotten, and those who turn to Google or Wikipedia can learn no more than the opinion expressed by many who knew little of her and followed the crowd: that she was a female hysteric who abused her boss in front of co-workers and got away with it. The civil servants determined to quench her power were misogynists almost to a man. Her female co-workers, apprehensive of disagreeing with their male bosses, moaned and gossiped about her reputation for haughty and bossy behaviour. Perhaps they had a point. Marcia, right from the start, complained that when they went on the road with the Prime Minister, the female staff of No. 10, behatted and high-heeled, were too well dressed and glamorous to be credible representatives of a Labour Prime Minister. These 'Garden Room Girls', the female typists who kept No. 10 running behind the scenes, many of whom had just like Marcia been privately educated and attended secretarial colleges, were rightly miffed.

Some men waited over thirty years until Harold and many of his Kitchen Cabinet had died and then released journals and diaries which focused on Marcia's sad private life and suggested that single-handedly she ruined Harold Wilson's chances of being remembered as a 'great' Prime Minister. His government had a whiff of corruption, and it was always blamed on Marcia. She was tall, blonde and powerful. 'Why did she have such a hold over Harold?' The assumption was that she was some historical Monica Lewinsky figure who turned a botched sexual encounter or two into a way of blackmailing the most powerful man in the land. It wasn't true of Lewinsky, and it wasn't what happened between Harold and Marcia. From the day they met in 1956 until the day Harold died forty years later, they were political partners who shared a passion for politics and supported each other totally. Both had enormous talents which complemented the other's and together they were a formidable power couple who gave their all to getting Labour elected and re-elected from 1964 to 1970 and twice in 1974. But in Labour Party history, there is no mention of the vital role played by Marcia Williams. Today, large numbers of clever and enthusiastic young people eager to make their political way become special advisers at No. 10 and play key roles advancing the power of those they work for, and frequently become politicians themselves. But Marcia Williams, who singlehandedly carved out a place for the political party to play an important part in Downing Street to complement the civil servants who dealt with the machinery of government, is completely forgotten.

It has become commonplace to hear politicians tell the public it's a great shame that UK Labour has never had a female leader. Conservatives point triumphantly to their three, and Labour wonder out loud why it hasn't happened for them, speculating on the reasons for this omission. They need to ask themselves why during the great years of successful 'all-women shortlists' and the arrival of the first women in the great offices of state (Foreign and Home

Secretaries) they have never understood or encouraged the unique skills women from every background can bring to the table. Some of those skills like housekeeping, organising accounting and public relations are still rubbished by male politicians who are only happy to accept female colleagues who think and work like the men they have replaced. Tony Blair was delighted to carry 101 female MPs with him into the Commons in 1997, but he was cheerfully sheepish a few years later when he admitted he couldn't work a washing machine, and his match for Marcia, Alastair Campbell, still refuses to perform any household duties at all. I suggest, as Mrs Harris did, that 'womanly' skills are still being ignored as a real contribution and 'acting up with the blokes' is not the right answer in the search for a female Labour leader. The very first time I arrived in Flood Street, Chelsea, to film Margaret Thatcher at home, her son Mark answered the door. She greeted me at the kitchen sink, scrubbing away at a pie dish with a Brillo pad. Then when I was about to leave and I mentioned that I was going home to my tiny twins in Yorkshire, she commanded Denis to drive me to King's Cross. I never forgot that.

Marcia Matilda Field, later Williams, occasionally Williams-Terry and finally and triumphantly Baroness Falkender of West Haddon, was for most of her adult life famous, even notorious, among those in the know. Inside the Westminster bubble, politicians, civil servants and journalists alike gasped and gossiped behind their hands about Marcia's supposed exploits. Readers of the new and important satirical magazine *Private Eye*, which began in 1961, gasped with amazement about her affairs. Could she really have concealed two pregnancies and produced two illegitimate sons ten months apart, fathered by the chief political correspondent of the *Daily Mail* while working as the Prime Minister's right-hand woman in No. 10? Well, it turned out she could. Joe Haines, head of Harold Wilson's press office, did the maths and reckoned that Daniel Williams-Terry, Marcia's second son, was conceived on board Britain's appropriately named warship HMS *Fearless* during the Rhodesia talks off Gibraltar in 1968. Pauline Windross, now a Huddersfield pensioner, recalls looking after both of Marcia's newborns who, just ten months apart, were smuggled into her care in Westminster apartments, while Marcia went back to work in Downing Street.

Marcia Williams was at the leading edge of a new group of talented professional women who began to emerge slowly in the second half of the twentieth century. She was cool, organised and very efficient. If she was doing the same job today, she would be hailed by admirers as 'a difficult woman', which is now a badge worn with pride by those who have made their way to the summit of their chosen career paths neatly sidestepping or clambering over the men on the route.

In October 1956, when she was hired by the Labour MP for Ormskirk, Harold Wilson, as his personal secretary, Marcia immediately became so much more. In six years, she deftly guided his rapid rise from his double starring role as chairman of the Public Accounts Committee and shadow Chancellor of the Exchequer to Prime Minister, where he served for nearly eight years. She took on the relationship between an MP and his constituents, solved problems, sorted injustices and strengthened the bond between them. She became Harold Wilson's bosom buddy and closest adviser and never really left his side again until he died nearly forty years later, suffering from colon cancer and dementia. Marcia worked for him and supported him to the end. She stood side by side with his widow Mary at his funeral.

Marcia died in 2019 – in a private nursing home, battered, broken by illness and virtually penniless. Four years later, no will nor probate declaration has been published, so we must assume her net worth was small. Ade Adenuga, who owns Newstead Lodge, told me that Marcia, who always had a story to tell, was popular with the other residents. He also enjoyed her company and had been hoping that Marcia would recover. She had promised him a lunch at the House of Lords if she could make it.

Her obituaries spoke of her power and her skill in dominating a Prime Minister, and many gave examples of her ability to bend the Prime Minister to her will. 'If only he could have rid himself of Marcia,' they mused, 'he would have been up there with Thatcher and Blair as one of the great Prime Ministers of the twentieth century.'

Except for a couple of carefully arranged and sympathetic television interviews fixed by Harold Wilson when he stood down as Prime Minister in 1976, one with Judith Chalmers for Thames Television and one with Austin Mitchell for Yorkshire Television, there was never any attempt to defend Marcia by anyone except Harold. She seems to have been universally feared or scorned by the people she worked with: civil servants, politicians and parliamentary staffers all had their tales to tell of her appalling behaviour, her hysteria and the way she bullied her boss and anyone else unlucky enough to get in her way.

Newspapers and radio and TV companies sent journalists and photographers to lay siege to her various houses and speculate endlessly about her activities and her relationship with the Prime Minister. She became a serial star of *Private Eye*, occupying more column inches than almost anyone else. In the magazine's topical index, entries for 'Falkender' take up three times as much space as the next subject, 'Falklands War'.

In 1974, fed up with what he saw as Marcia's totally unjustified persecution by the press, Harold nominated Marcia for a peerage. The *Eye*, in homage to Uri Geller the king of spoon bending, dubbed her 'Forkbender' and it stuck. It seemed her only publicly acknowledged achievements were twisting outcomes rather than spoons, and winning libel suits.

Today, few people have heard of Marcia. Those few may have had their memories jogged by Sinead Matthews playing the part of adviser to the Prime Minister in a cameo role in the Netflix series *The Crown*.

There is a scene in Downing Street just after the Aberfan disaster on 21 October 1966, when slagheaps in the mining village erupted and slid down, burying the village school. In total, 144 people were killed, including 116 children.

Harold Wilson, frustrated, explains to Marcia that the Queen is refusing to visit the site of the tragedy immediately because she feels that her appearance in a small Welsh village would deflect attention away from the tragedy and on to her. There is, he says, nothing he can do about it.

The Crown's Marcia is seen screaming angrily at her boss, urging him to explain the rights and wrongs of the situation to the monarch. The fictional lines Marcia speaks in the show are based on her reputation for abusing and controlling the Prime Minister.

'You're pathetic! You disgust me! If you ever want to be a real leader, a real man, a real socialist, you're going to have to grow some balls!'

'Ah yes, Forkbender!' *Private Eye* readers will have recalled. But what viewers were watching was a fictional encounter based on reports mostly from journalist Joe Haines, who was head of Wilson's press office in the 1970s, of Marcia's intemperate behaviour much later in her political career.

Marcia's brief appearance in *The Crown* encapsulates everything she had become infamous for in the 1970s. Although she was sixteen years his junior, Marcia was said to exercise an incredible degree of control over Wilson. She shouted, screamed and abused him in private, according to Haines in *Glimmers of Twilight*, published in 2003.

There is no doubt that from the beginning of her career in Downing Street in 1964, she interfered, she stuck to her guns and disagreed firmly and positively with anyone who got in her way. But reports of her behaviour were frequently tainted with sexism. In the Labour governments of the 1960s, her enemies were misogynistic civil servants who saw her as a super-gatekeeper protecting Harold Wilson from the long-established relationship between them and a new Prime Minister. But like her or not, everyone in the 1960s saw her as incredibly smart and efficient and the first woman to wield real power in Downing Street. So, what changed in the 1970s and ignited the public bonfires of abuse? Her huge reputation for hysteria and out-of-control behaviour – bolstered, I will argue, by large quantities of drugs – began only after the arrival of her secret sons and the rapid departure of their father.

Reports of her erratic behaviour in the 1970s are legion. Lord (Robin) Butler, who has been private secretary to five Prime Ministers, Cabinet Secretary and head of the civil service, recalls that at the beginning of his civil service career in the 1970s, Marcia worked hard to get him sacked and thrown out of Downing Street. That would have finished his amazing career almost before it began. Even today in his eighties, Robin Butler remembers what a great nuisance Marcia could be:

> I established an easy personal relationship with Harold and with Bernard [Donoughue] because he was easy to establish a relationship with, and Joe Haines too. I hadn't known him before but that worked fine, so we were a group now. The political side – Marcia and Albert Murray [who had been the MP for Gravesend but lost his seat in 1970 and was made a peer in the Lavender List] – they were always a bit separate. We were dealing with the policy and they were dealing with the politics, but from the beginning Marcia was a bloody nuisance and such a bloody nuisance that I could hardly believe it.
>
> She would arrange commitments and engagements for Harold without any concern for what was in his official diary, clashing engagements and so on, using the Prime Minister's car when she wanted to go shopping or pick up her children from school and generally behaving in a way that for me, aged thirty-four and a slightly idealistic ingenuous civil servant, seemed to be completely shocking and of course all the more shocking because it was in contrast to the very austere days of Ted Heath, when everything was like a gentleman's club.

One wonders whether such unconventional, forthright behaviour in the high-stress environment of Downing Street would have drawn the same criticism if it came from a man.

Civil servants in the 1960s and '70s were as famous for their 're-served' behaviour as they were for their bowler hats. Marcia mentioned after her first visit to Downing Street that they all assembled mid-afternoon to drink tea from china cups. If you've seen Bill Nighy in *Living*, you get the picture.

A report from the Social Mobility Commission in 2021 opened with:

> Emotional detachment and understated self-presentation are seen as the behavioural hallmarks of senior civil servants, perhaps in contrast to their political leaders. But this 'neutral' behaviour can be both alienating and intimidating for those from working class backgrounds. Those working in Ministers' private offices or who have led during a national crisis, for example, tend to get promoted, often helped by senior colleagues with similar cultural and socio-economic backgrounds. Those left behind tend to be in operational roles – where bottlenecks occur and progress is slower or non-existent. The barriers to advancement are there from the start.

And here was Marcia, entering a largely male world side by side and perfectly in step with Prime Minister Harold Wilson as he led Britain in the 1960s and '70s. How could this be? Was she black-mailing him? Had something happened between them that he was frightened could be revealed? What kind of man was he to allow a woman such control? Who was this woman, the very first to wield real power in 10 Downing Street?

2

When Harold Met Marcia

The story of Harold and Marcia and their special relationship began on 23 April 1956 in the Harcourt Room, a gracious Palace of Westminster dining room overlooking the River Thames. Today it's called the Churchill Room, and the walls are adorned with paintings of Britain and Europe by Winston Churchill himself. Back in the 1950s, however, the space was dark and sombre, the river boats glittering through the windows and Commons mice and the odd rat scuttling along the skirting boards on their well-trodden route from the river to the kitchens and back.

Newly married Marcia Williams – aged twenty-four and armed with a history degree from Queen Mary and a shorthand typist qualification from St Godric's in Hampstead – had just begun work at Transport House, Labour Party HQ, headed by General Secretary Morgan Phillips. Eager to get stuck in, Marcia was tasked, along with the more-experienced staffer Irene Litherland, with arranging and overseeing a dinner for the Labour Party's top men and a distinguished international delegation. Unbeknown to anyone else in the room, Marcia Williams had been in contact several times with one of the Labour politicians present that night – the shadow Chancellor Harold Wilson – but, intriguingly, he wasn't aware of this.

At Transport House, the beating heart of the Labour Party, Marcia shared an office with three other women – two were older and would have been regarded as right of centre in the party, but the third was more like Marcia, both in age and the fact that she enjoyed talking about her left-wing beliefs.

Morgan Phillips watched everyone carefully and made sure that his workers and the policies that came out of Transport House firmly supported the right wing of the party and its leader Clement Attlee.

Marcia, on the other hand, confesses that she was a great admirer of Aneurin 'Nye' Bevan, the Welsh politician who had spearheaded the founding of the National Health Service:

> He was a hero figure to all of us, particularly younger members of the party. We admired and idolised him but were never sure what he would do. There was a sense among many people that he didn't have the qualities needed to put his ideas into practice. We were looking round for someone else who could fulfil that role.

And Marcia felt that she had spotted just that person: Harold Wilson, the Lancashire MP who had just come back from a nationwide tour of local Labour Parties across Britain. With the meticulous hard work he had become known for in head office, Wilson had come up with a plan to reorganise and secure the future of local parties. He'd also attracted a nationwide army of supporters who liked the young MP who had made the effort to visit them.

Marcia had also heard that Wilson had been a successful civil servant during the war, and even had head office approval for the work he did as a junior minister in the Ministry of Works and then in the Department of Trade in Clement Attlee's post-war government.

So, it's safe to say that young Marcia had a bit of a crush on Harold, the ambitious left-wing politician sixteen years her senior. When she'd been at school, she'd written loads of letters to the American film stars she and her friend Ann Cauldwell had admired on their weekly visits to the cinema in Northampton. Ronald Reagan, Gary Cooper and Frank Sinatra had all had letters from Marcia requesting autographs and telling them how much she'd enjoyed their performances.

Marcia decided to put her letter-writing skills to good use in her work life too and began writing to Harold Wilson – but she did so anonymously.

She knew that her boss Morgan Phillips was a very staunch supporter of Hugh Gaitskell and all the other MPs on the right wing of the party. 'He knew how to manage the party and keep it in line with what Gaitskell wanted.'

But Marcia thought that there was a deliberate putsch against Harold in head office, beginning with an attempt to keep him off the organisation subcommittee.

So she began sending infrequent notes to Harold warning him of 'certain things that were happening' which might affect his progress. 'I know what I did was wrong,' she confessed, 'but I wanted to see the left and Harold succeed.'

Eight years before he won the 1964 general election and became Britain's first Labour Prime Minister in thirteen years, Harold Wilson was chosen and helped on his way by a young and recently graduated shorthand typist who spotted his talent and acted on it.

It was many years later when she told Harold what she had done. 'Harold afterwards joked that he wondered who this person could be, and how were they so well informed. He did not know any of this when he appointed me as his secretary in October 1956.'

So Harold Wilson and Marcia Williams met officially for the first time at that dinner on 23 April 1956, immortalised by both of them as '23456', according to Joe Haines, the head of Wilson's press office in the 1970s, who claims Marcia froze with fear if he taunted her with the memorable number.

That was the night Marcia and Harold were present at the famous falling out between leading politicians from the Labour Party and the two most important men in the Soviet Union.

Communist Party First Secretary Nikita Khrushchev and his sidekick Soviet Premier Nikolai Bulganin were on a visit to Britain as guests of the Conservative government. It was such an important event that historians dubbed it 'the crossroads of the twentieth century'.

The Russians had arrived by warship and were then escorted around the country in limousines, trains and a new and glamorous Vickers Viscount aircraft. They were entertained by mayors and business leaders. They met the Queen and members of the royal family and visited important and successful industries. There were always British Cabinet ministers at their sides, entertaining and explaining. By the evening of 23 April, everyone on both sides agreed that the tour was going well.

The Russians were trying to give a good impression of what the Soviet Union had to offer the world. 'Socialism carried on the wings of Soviet science,' explained Khrushchev.

The British government made sure their tour was jam-packed

with events designed to show off the best of Britain. There are hundreds of pages of transcripts of speeches and conversations at all the events. There are also films, radio broadcasts and interviews.

But the celebration on the evening of 23 April was something different. The Russians were to be hosted in the dining room at the House of Commons by leading figures from the Labour Party, including the leader, Hugh Gaitskell, as well as George Brown and Harold Wilson.

Wilson, the shadow Chancellor, was keenly interested in Russia and Russian technological advances and he had been a frequent visitor to the Soviet Union.

In 1946, MPs' pay had been increased to £1,000 a year with no staff or travel allowances. It was part of an MP's job to raise the money to pay for their travel back and forth to their constituency and to pay anyone they wanted to employ, so Harold Wilson had a side hustle. He worked for Montague L. Meyer, a successful timber importing company, and he often went to Russia on Meyer's business. He worked out of their London offices in the mornings and went off to the House of Commons for the afternoon and evening. This practice was quite standard among MPs at this time. They were lawyers and other professionals in the morning, and they arrived in the Commons in time for prayers at 2.30 p.m. Shirley Summerskill, then MP for Halifax, recalls working as an accident and emergency doctor at Westminster Hospital in the mornings and running along the streets to the Commons after lunch.

The Westminster dinner on 23 April 1956 was the only opportunity the opposition were given to be alone with the Russians during their ten-day visit.

Party boss Morgan Phillips oversaw the evening, but he handed over the organisation of the event to Irene Litherland and the office's newbie, Marcia Williams.

Ben Pimlott, in his biography of Harold Wilson, said that Phillips kept tight personal control of everything in the Labour Party from his office in Transport House, driving policies firmly to the right of the central reservation. No British communists were to get a look in. Everything in the party must be firmly fixed and Phillips was fixer-in-chief.

Irene and Marcia went about their work, adjusting place settings and showing guests to their tables, but as so often happens at events in the Commons, not all the guests turned up. Phillips instructed 'the girls' to grab the spare seats, get out their notebooks and keep a shorthand record of everything that was said.

Marcia recalls:

It was a tough assignment, and I was frozen with fear one minute and covered with nervous perspiration the next. Harold Wilson, who sat at the end of the top table a short distance away from my seat, sensed my nervousness and was extremely sympathetic. I never forgot his kindness that evening.

CIA reports made public fifty years later described the dinner as a fiasco. Khrushchev antagonised the Labour leaders by repeating charges he had made in India that Britain and France had urged Hitler to attack Russia. Labour leaders replied with a plea for the immediate release of Soviet Social Democrats and trade unionists who were in custody. Drink was taken enthusiastically by both sides, and Khrushchev roared that he found it much easier to talk to the Conservative UK government than the British Labour Party.

A member of the shadow Cabinet, George Brown, who already had a solid reputation as a 'world-class' imbiber, began picking on Khrushchev's student son who was sitting at his table. 'You don't always agree with your father about everything, do you?' he encouraged the lad.

Fuelled by anger and even more alcohol, the row raged on until just before midnight, when Labour leader Gaitskell rose to speak. Even though the atmosphere was tense, Gaitskell raised the topic of antisemitism in the Soviet Union. He asked Khrushchev to consider the release of Social Democrats imprisoned in Eastern Europe.

'Why should we care what happens to enemies of the working class?' Khrushchev bawled. The evening ended in total disarray and leaked reports of the unhappy event featured in newspapers around the world.

Some months later, Marcia's detailed shorthand notes of the chaotic dinner were reproduced in the *Daily Express*. Someone had leaked them for £500.

Reports of Harold and Marcia's interactions when they left the dinner vary, with some saying that she left the Commons to wait for the night bus to Golders Green, and that Harold saw her in the queue and stopped to give her a lift on his way home to Hampstead Garden Suburb. A man called George Caunt had a different tale to tell.

Caunt was an election agent working out of Transport House on the night of the Russian dinner. He was later to become the organiser of Harold Wilson's general election campaigns, employed at 10 Downing Street and a part-time member of the inner circle. He was Wilson's election agent in 1964, did odd jobs for Harold and worked closely with him and with Marcia. He was awarded a OBE for his efforts in Harold Wilson's 1970 resignation honours. Caunt fancied himself as something of a historian. He had written a short series called *Essex Yesterdays: Holidays into History*. Like others who were close to Wilson and Marcia, he decided to write a memoir of their time together.

On 23 February 1977, the front page of the *Sun* newspaper was headlined 'Marcia and Secrets ... the proof'. Caunt, like many others, had become interested in the reports of endless rows between the recently retired Prime Minister and Marcia and had begun researching and writing a book on their relationship. *The Sun* had cherry-picked some accusations from the manuscript.

Caunt claimed that Wilson allowed Marcia to see secret and classified documents when she worked for him but without the correct security clearances for staff at No. 10. He highlighted a casual approach to paperwork, with 'secret files scattered about', and protests from Derek Mitchell, then chief secretary and the head civil servant in Downing Street, that Mrs Williams was being given access to highly confidential information without a proper security clearance.

I immediately began a search for the Caunt book but found it was never published. Like so many others before and since, he had sold an extract from an unpublished manuscript to a newspaper but never completed the book. George Caunt died in the 1980s and his widow sold his papers to Leeds University on the understanding that the boxes could not be opened for thirty years. They had remained unopened until I applied to see them in 2021.

Caunt had never completed his book, but he had done some serious research on Marcia, including his version of events from 23456, the night Harold and Marcia met.

'The meeting ended in confusion and Wilson offered Marcia

Williams a lift in his car, and that night began an affair which was to last 5/6 years,' Caunt wrote.

Caunt said that Harold had watched Marcia diligently taking shorthand notes of the speeches, went up to her and introduced himself and offered her a lift home. It's easy to imagine how exciting that car journey must have been. A disappointed British politician who loved visiting Russia and admired the Soviet Union's scientific advancements, and an ambitious young woman just out of university who already deeply admired the politician and was writing him anonymous letters, revealing her boss Morgan Phillips's eagerness to keep the British Labour Party firmly to the right under its leader Clement Attlee. It seems that the car journey was a long one. There was much to discuss.

'Marcia Williams returned late, and they were both worried about Mr Williams waiting up for her. They agreed on a secret sign at the executive committee meeting the next morning (sugar in the saucer) if Mr Williams had been awake and asked questions,' Caunt claimed.

Caunt was convinced that Harold and Marcia had begun an impassioned affair on 23456 and he went to some lengths to provide some evidence:

By the autumn of 1956, Wilson was looking for a secretary and a secret arrangement was come to between the two that after the 1956 Labour conference, she would leave the Labour Party to become his secretary ...

Wilson was at Meyer's and Mrs Williams operated from there until 1960 when he became chair of the Public Accounts Committee at the House of Commons with a large office. Mrs Williams moved in ... After the 1959 general election, Mrs Williams was at the House and seen regularly by many people ...

Often the two would arrive at the Strangers' Cafeteria in the House of Commons at about 7 p.m. and go over correspondence etc. There was a lot of gossip and scandal at this time as she always walked closely behind him, and they always sat at a table for two.

In 1957, she became very fat, particularly her hips, and an outspoken woman asked her when it was coming. Mrs Williams blew her top at the suggestion. Sometime later, probably six months to a year, she reappeared and was quite slim. Since then, she has been on a rigid diet.

And there ended the report. Many who worked in and around the Commons in the 1950s believed that Harold and Marcia were an item following that fateful dinner on 23456. They had a close and intimate relationship which was due to last a lifetime. Bernard Donoughue, whose *Downing Street Diary* was an important source of information about Marcia's day-to-day behaviour when they both worked together in the 1970s Labour government, told me that Bill Housden, who had been Harold Wilson's loyal driver over the years, had said that he had often delivered Harold to Marcia's home and picked him up much later. When I asked Margarete Field, Marcia's sister-in-law, whether she thought Harold and Marcia had had an affair in the early days of their relationship, she laughed bitterly and said, 'Well, what do you think?'

The most intriguing hint to what might have happened in 1957 appears in Richard Crossman's *Backbench Diaries*. He writes on 29 March 1957:

To dinner last night and Harold turned up trumps. To my annoyance, having said he would come early, he arrived forty-five minutes late, but he melted my heart when he explained that this was because he had been with his secretary who had just had a nervous breakdown. He had spent twenty minutes on the phone with her husband. All this was really endearing since afterwards he had said, 'Take my mind off her for God's sake by discussing pensions,' so I did.

Marcia believed that everything said about her – the accusations, the allegations, the libels which dogged her for all her lifetime – had one root cause. She was a woman in a society not ready for a woman in power, and if not in power, certainly not at the right hand of the man who was.

3

Marcia: The Beginnings

Marcia's parents lived in the Northamptonshire village of Long Buckby. Marcia was born at home on 10 March 1932, the third and final child of Harry Field and his wife Dorothy Matilda Cowley. Marcia had an elder sister Peggy, and a brother Tony. Just a month after Marcia's birth, her mother travelled by bus to the Daventry Registry Office to record her new daughter's arrival.

When Marcia died in 2019, many of the obituaries reported that 'from an early age' she had told people that her mother was the illegitimate daughter of King Edward VII, the son and heir of Queen Victoria. The prince was known to his family as Bertie and to many of his subjects as 'Dirty Bertie'. People heard tales of his endless womanising, and even today the names of his three main mistresses – Lillie Langtry, Daisy Warwick and Alice Keppel – have a familiar ring. Alice Keppel is now remembered more as the great-grandmother of Queen Camilla. King Charles and Queen Camilla seem amused and proud of the relationship between their great-grandparents. Charles, with the help of the jeweller Wartski, bought a tiara that once belonged to Camilla's great-grandmother. He had the diamonds remade into a necklace and earrings and gave them to her as a gift. Perhaps it's easy to understand why a young Marcia might be enthralled by the idea of such goings-on in her own family history.

The story of Edward VII must have been a tale told to Marcia and her siblings by their mother. Did she believe it? Marcia's friend from Northampton High School Ann Cauldwell had never heard mention of it, but when Marcia became a public figure as the close confidant and political secretary to the Prime Minister, other people did hear about it, and the possibility of royal ancestry followed her through her life.

When Marcia was made a peer in 1974, Anthony J. Camp, a senior figure in the Society of Genealogists, looked more closely at the story.

Marcia Williams, who took the surname Falkender by deed poll and received a life peerage as Baroness Falkender of West Haddon in 1974, mentioned that her mother was said to have been an un-acknowledged child of Edward VII. Apparently an aide-de-camp named Falkender obliged him by claiming to be the child's father. No further details of the claimed liaison are known, and Camp concluded that the story appears 'to have been invented to hide the humble status of the family'.

Marcia's mother, Dorothy Matilda Falkender Cowley, was born illegitimately at 151 Battersea Park Road, Wandsworth, on 8 March 1902. She was the daughter of Jane Cowley (née Woodcock), a cleaner. Jane informed the registrar of the birth on 25 April 1902. Her daughter was baptised 'Dorothy Cowley, daughter of Jane Cowley, of Battersea, London', at West Haddon, Northamptonshire, on 7 September 1902.

Marcia's grandmother Jane was also illegitimate herself, being born before her parents, John Woodcock and Matilda Townsend, wed. She was baptised Edith Jane Townsend in West Haddon on 12 July 1874, and her parents married in the village on 17 August 1876. As Edith Jane Woodcock, she had married John Cowley in West Haddon on 19 January 1893. The couple had one child, Lucy Kathleen, in 1894, but the infant died shortly afterwards and was registered in the surname Cowley-York. From 1885 to 1897, John Cowley, sometimes called John York Cowley, served in the Royal Artillery, but there is no record of his later history. Meanwhile, Jane Cowley had left John and travelled to south London, where in March 1901 she was living in one room at 151 Battersea Park Road and describing herself as single, aged twenty-five and working as a cleaner. Her later history is also vague, and she is untraceable after the birth of Dorothy in 1902.

As Camp uncovered, there was only one person called Falkender living in the London area at the time of Dorothy Cowley's conception in June 1901: one William Falkender, who on 31 March 1901 was a lance sergeant in the 3rd Coldstream Guards and a patient in the Military Hospital at Kidbrooke in Kent. He was single, aged twenty-three. Born William Thomas Falkender on 6 June 1878, he was a labourer who he had enlisted in the Guards in July 1896. He was promoted to sergeant in 1902 and, having remained in England throughout his service, was discharged as medically unfit in October 1903. His parents lived at Wallsend, Northumberland, and he returned there, subsequently marrying and dying in Gateshead in 1949. Whether he had a connection with Dorothy Cowley or Edward VII is untraceable.

By the time she was nine, Dorothy was living with her grandmother Matilda Woodcock in West Haddon. The 1911 census recorded that Dorothy was born at '16 Battersea Road'. The widowed

Matilda, who brought Dorothy up, took in washing at home and died in 1929.

Marcia's parents, Dorothy Matilda Cowley and Harry Field, had married by banns (her father's name and occupation being left blank in the entry) at All Saints, West Haddon, on 19 April 1926. Harry, born on 12 November 1903, was a 22-year-old bricklayer from the village, son of Harry Field, also a bricklayer. The couple's next appearance in a census was in 1939, when they were living with their three children – Peggy, Marcia and Anthony – at 46 Norfolk Street, Glossop, Derbyshire. Harry had risen to be a brickworks manager. The family moved back to Northamptonshire, where Harry built quite a few of the local brick houses. He died at the family home, 2 Hardys Lane, West Haddon, on 29 December 1972. He left £24,000 to his wife, who then moved to London to live with Marcia. Dorothy died at Marcia's home in Westminster in June 1978, by which time Marcia had lived to fulfil her mother's dreams of royal connections by becoming a member of the House of Lords.

The Fields seemed to be a modest and hard-working family. Throughout his life, Marcia's father moved slowly from brickie to builder and, before his retirement, had built several houses in Northamptonshire.

His children were hard-working and successful too. Tony won a scholarship to Northampton Grammar School, where a couple of years behind him Bernard Donoughue was also a student. Marcia and her elder sister Peggy were clever enough to get scholarships to Northampton High School, the best girls' school in the area. Part of the Girls' Day School Trust and still very well regarded these days, fees in the Senior School are £17,419.20 per year including lunches.

Northampton High School was formed in 1878 with the daunting name the 'Northampton Middle-Class Girls' School', so Peggy and Marcia must have known when they started there that they were beginning their climb up the social ladder. Lord Donoughue, who also grew up in Northampton, wrote in the preface to his diaries in 2005:

> I remember as a young teenager frequently seeing her striding into Northampton's Derngate bus station, from where she travelled daily from the posh Northampton High School for Girls to her village some ten miles north of the town. Then Marcia Field, daughter of a local builder, she struck me – admittedly younger and poorer than her and distinctly uncouth – as very tall, well dressed, very determined and perhaps having social aspirations a cut above most of my raucous Northamptonshire associates. She never mixed with our group of teenagers noisily gossiping and flirting in the dirty bus station.

Northampton High School was a direct grant school where girls who took the local scholarship (which became the eleven-plus) and those who lived round Northampton town were educated for free.

Being a direct grant school, it also had many fee-paying private pupils including Marcia's friend Ann Cauldwell, who recalls:

> In our day it was roughly half and half paying pupils and scholarship girls. My father was earning about £300 a year as a curate. It was seven guineas a term and my sister started in the kindergarten at five. She went right through from the age of five – I don't know how they managed to pay it, but they did.

Ann's father had been a Congregational minister in Slaithwaite in Yorkshire and then moved to Kettering, where he was asked to stand for Labour in the general election. He refused the offer, and the family moved on to Northampton in 1943 when she was eleven. In those days, the school was in an old vicarage in Derngate right in the centre of town.

I suppose in the senior school there were about sixty-four girls in each year right up to taking the school certificate, so most girls left school when they were fifteen or sixteen after taking that exam. Marcia and I were in the same class from the day I arrived at my new school. We were just twelve and autograph collection was popular with all of us. Here's what Marcia wrote in my book nearly eighty years ago:

> When the golden sun is sinking,
> And your mind from care is free.
> When of others you are thinking,
> Will you sometimes think of me?

Because I was a town girl, most of my school friends were girls who lived in the town. The Fields lived in the village of West Haddon. Very few people in those days had telephones or cars so you couldn't get out into the country easily, you couldn't speak to people on the phone, so my friends were in the town, and the other girls were scattered in different villages.

I probably became aware of Peggy first because Peggy was two years older than us. I got to know Marcia and she became a close friend when we got to the sixth form.

There were very few people in the sixth form – only about

twelve girls would go up each year into the sixth form and Marcia and I were the only two doing geography so of course I got to know her very well because of that. We also did English and history together and that's when we started to go to the cinema, sometimes with Peggy, but usually it was just Marcia and me. We were writing to all the film stars and getting all their autographed pictures. During the war, I sometimes went to the pictures two or three times a week. By the time I knew Marcia, we were both living in the country and there were not that many buses. The last bus to the village where I lived left Northampton at 9.30 p.m., so I am not quite sure how we saw *Gone with the Wind*, whether we saw it on an afternoon, or on a Saturday.

I loved anything with Tyrone Power in it, or Gary Cooper. I suppose it was the film star rather than the film. I loved anything with Elizabeth Taylor because she was the same age as me and we both had black hair and blue eyes and both loved riding. We wrote to so many film stars – we must have written to twenty or thirty, all the film stars of the time during the war. We asked for autographed photographs from all the stars of the 1940s. We didn't write to English ones, just American ones. We both had autograph books and collected them locally as well. It's about all there was to do in those days; there was no television.

Marcia came to tea for my seventeenth birthday. Tony brought her on the back of his motor bike.

Marcia and I read a book about three girls whose wartime job was working the canals, delivering fuel and things from canal barges. Marcia always joked that that's what she would end up doing. I was in love with the navy by then – I had a naval uncle and I used to go and stay with them, and I met some of the gorgeous naval officers who had their own yachts, so I became hooked on sailing. Marcia always used to joke that I would have my yacht and she would have her barge on the canal.

If you were going to university, you stayed on to take the entrance exam in the third year. I went off to London to St Barts to train to be a nurse and I didn't see Marcia again. We didn't have a chance to experience high life. I remember sometimes when we went to the cinema in Northampton, we went to the cafe in the cinema and had Heinz spaghetti on toast for our tea. Nothing exciting ever seemed to happen in Northampton.

I was amazed years later when I discovered what had happened to Marcia. There was a picture of her visiting South Africa, they went on a naval frigate or cruiser. I wrote to her at 10 Downing Street. But in all honesty, she might never have received the letter. I do wish I had made more strenuous efforts to keep in touch.

Ann's recollections of Marcia paint a picture of a fun young woman, with a burning passion for film stars and their autographs and a desire to live the high life. Such feelings were to stay with Marcia for the rest of her life. Her interest in film stars and their autographs turned into a lifelong love of movies and the theatre. In her time in Downing Street, she was always inviting entrepreneurs and the stars they worked with to events, and she certainly understood and was very interested in the social advancement that being made a peer could bring. For a girl who joked that she might find work on a coal barge on the canals after she left school, it seems she understood from an early age that getting on included rising up the social hierarchy.

In her second book *Downing Street in Perspective*, Marcia wrote a short chapter justifying her own introduction to the House of Lords on 23 July 1974.

As she knelt down, the Lord Chancellor Elwyn Jones whispered in her ear, 'It's not such good fun as HMS *Fearless*, is it?' The newly introduced peer then bowed to the throne.

> When I did this, I noticed that a number of Privy Counsellors had availed themselves of their privilege of sitting on the steps of the throne. Among them was Harold Wilson.
>
> I left the chamber, as I did so Eric Varley who was standing just inside the doorway – he too had been sitting on the steps of the throne during the ceremony – gave me a big hug and a kiss and I went out into the corridor where Thomas Balogh and Gerald Kaufman were also waiting for me. I remember those moments and the faces and words of good friends from the early years particularly well – and my dear mother bursting with pride and in floods of tears.

For two women who believed themselves the daughter and granddaughter of King Edward VII, it must have been a wonderful turn of events.

4

Harold: The Beginnings

In Britain today, the name Ethel, originally shortened from Ethelreda, is very rare. Out of favour even for your grandma. Only one in every 70,000 girls born in the UK in 2021 was named Ethel and there is little sign of a revival. At the beginning of the twentieth century, Ethel was the sixth most popular name for your baby girl.

When I arrived in Yorkshire from New Zealand in 1968 with Austin and baby twins to meet my father-in-law Richard and his wife Ethel for the first time, Ethel had already faded into a great name for a granny – the Mitchells' Ethel was Mary to her friends and Mummy to her family. Richard was a heavy-set, brooding, say-little kind of bloke. He had been head dyer at Bradford Dyers, made redundant in his late fifties and never worked again. The redundancy had sunk him in bitter misery, and he never succeeded in climbing out of it. He was sad and angry and overweight. I knew him for twenty years and he said little. Austin's mother was completely different. Busy, bright, smart and clever. Her eyes lit up and she sparkled the minute Austin walked into a room. There was a very strong bond between them. When I started working on the story of Marcia and Harold, I was reminded vividly of Austin's mother, Ethel Mary Butterworth. There were clear resonances with Harold's mother, Ethel Seddon. Harold's father, Herbert Wilson, had also been a head dyer but in Huddersfield just over ten miles from Shipley where Richard Mitchell was unemployed. Herbert was described as 'provincial' and 'close to his roots' and had also lost his job in his fifties.

The two Ethels were tough northern women, strong and very clever with it. If they'd been born just a few decades later, they would have been successful in business, heads of schools or hospitals or big banks. Even MPs or a Prime Minister. But they were brilliant brains and organisers born at a time when Britain had little use for smart women. Instead, both women cherished their academically clever sons and passionately encouraged their scholarly achievements. As Ben Pimlott said of Harold, he was 'a family project in whom all hope was invested'. It was the same for Austin.

Ethel Wilson, who'd never been out of Britain, amazed her family and neighbours when Harold was ten by taking him out of school for a year and setting off on the RMS *Esperance Bay* for western Australia to visit her brother, also Harold, who had emigrated to the gold mines of Kalgoorlie. Their father, William had travelled out to live with his son, and Ethel was keen for her young Harold to meet them both. Ethel's husband stayed back at home, looked after by their daughter, seventeen-year-old Marjorie.

Harold loved his visit to Australia. His relatives lived on a small farm and he walked a mile to school every day with his young cousins. He saw Australian country life in the raw, and learned to watch out for poisonous snakes and tarantulas.

Before he left the UK, Harold had visited London with his dad and famously had his photo taken on the steps of 10 Downing Street.

Now he was meeting his uncle Harold who was a politician in the Western Australia state Parliament. So, at age ten, young Harold got his first close-up experience of politics in the family, and he announced to his proud mother on the boat back to England that he was going to be an MP – and possibly even Prime Minister – when he grew up.

On his return to the UK, Harold wrote off eagerly to children's newspapers and magazines with tales of his adventures in the southern hemisphere. They were politely rejected, but his schoolteachers were very impressed by his efforts. Harold constructed a two-hour presentation (complete with visual aids) about his adventures abroad and delivered it individually to every class in the school.

When it came to moving on to secondary school, both Harold and Austin passed their exams with flying colours, acquired very formal school uniforms and went off to the grammar schools. Harold attended Royds Hall in Huddersfield; Austin went to Bingley Grammar in Bradford. Every time I drove Austin's mother to visit another daughter-in-law in Keighley, she would grin with excitement when we passed the school and point it out to me with pride. 'Here we are,' she said joyously, 'the Eton of the north.'

So, both sons had fulfilled their mother's dreams. They had followed the clear path of the brightest and the best Yorkshire lads. Meticulous hard work and attention to detail were key characteristics. Two Cubs followed by a pair of dedicated Scouts. Harold loved his Hornby trains and his Meccano set. Austin kept notebook after notebook of spider writing recording the date, time, lens, shutter setting and weather conditions for every photograph he ever took. In the past, this kind of industrious application to duty and the success which followed was always put down to the role of the grammar schools. Smart lads enabled by their trained brains to climb up from modest Yorkshire homes to a 'county major', unlocking the gates to university. No one has ever given the credit to those clever mums in search of a project.

Austin's mum explained to me the way things worked before A-levels were invented. The county major was abolished in the early 1960s but had been a bursary for those with the very best exam results. It paid for Austin to go to Manchester University, and Harold delighted his mum by getting into Jesus College, Oxford, with some of his fees paid.

These mums gave everything they had to the successful moulding of their precious sons. These women weren't encouraged to work outside the home, so their lad was their project. Through all the years of Herbert Wilson's unemployment, there was no hint of a suggestion that Ethel should go out to work. Ethel Mitchell's highest paid achievement was a part-time job on a stall in Bradford market.

When Harold was vying to be Labour leader a couple of decades later, his back story wasn't quite up to scratch with the party's other high-flyers. There was a ferocious pecking order. Apparently, Jesus was near the bottom of the list of desirable Oxford colleges. Roy Jenkins, Anthony Crosland, Denis Healey and Hugh Gaitskell were Balliol, Trinity, Balliol and New College in that order. Jesus was OK if you were Welsh or, whisper it behind your hand, 'provincial', but the epithet most used against Harold by the Labour glitterati was 'left wing'.

The mums who gave everything to turn their sons into politicians had other vital roles to fulfil. A bright lad was a lifetime's occupation. I rocked with laughter when my husband first told me that every Friday afternoon, for the four years he was a student in Manchester, he had wrapped his used underwear in brown paper and taken it to the post office to return to his mother for laundering. Clean and fresh, neatly wrapped and regular as clockwork, it would arrive back at his hall of residence on Monday morning. It is a treasured Mitchell family joke.

In January 1934, Harold Wilson wrote a note home to his mother included with his laundry: 'I think that for the first fortnight I shall just send my collars, hankies, vests pants and socks. The reason there are so many hankies is that I have a bad cold.'

Back then, it seems there was nothing an ambitious northern mum wouldn't turn her hand to, to promote the cause of her brilliant son.

When Harold joined the Cabinet, Ethel Wilson said, 'My brother is an honourable, my son is a right honourable, what more could a woman ask?'

Ethel Wilson died in 1957, less than a year after Marcia and Harold got together, so she was never to know he became Prime Minister. Harold said sadly, 'I found I couldn't believe, and I think I am a fairly rational kind of man, that death was the end of my mother.'

When Austin won the Grimsby by-election in 1977 on the same night as Labour lost Ashfield, a safe seat, with a 20 per cent swing to the Tories, Margaret Thatcher dubbed Ashfield the 'greatest by-election victory ever', but it was a proud and delighted Mary Mitchell who was pictured on the front of *The Times* outside the Commons with her grinning son and me the following Monday.

The Wilson family, just like the Mitchells, regarded the patriarch's unemployment as though it was a family disgrace and hid it from the neighbours. In autumn 1932, Harold's dad at long last found a job. But it meant that the Wilsons had to move to the other side of the Pennines. Herbert became the new chief chemist at Brotherton's

Chemical Works at Bromborough on the Wirral, just across the water from Liverpool. Harold became a pupil at the brand-new Wirral Grammar and was the school's first sixth-former. During a break in revision one day, he went down to meet his dad at the recreation park by the chemical works and caught sight of a young woman playing tennis. She was dressed in white and bathed in gold by the sun. When he was asked years later if it had been love at first sight, Harold said, 'It really was you know. She looked lovely in white.'

Harold went out and bought a tennis racquet. Three weeks later, he announced he was going to marry Gladys Mary Baldwin, the daughter of a Congregational minister from Diss in Norfolk. She was amused by this. Their engagement lasted six years. It's possible that Harold, always practical and efficient, had in his pocket a list of predicted lifetime achievements ending with Prime Minister, and acquiring a suitable wife would have been near the top. He was certainly keen to include Gladys, who later became Mary, in the Wilson family circle. In letters home to his parents from university, he regularly asked if they had seen her. Had they invited her round for tea? Would they bring her with them if they decided to come down to visit him in Oxford?

Gladys Mary was not at all interested in politics. She loved poetry and the English countryside. She was later to become a close friend of the poet John Betjeman, who was to become Poet Laureate when Harold was Prime Minister in 1972. There is a polite handwritten note from Mary to Marcia in the Wilson papers at the Bodleian Library asking that Sir John Betjeman be invited as Mary's guest to the Trooping the Colour. She said it was fine to invite Lady Betjeman as well if protocol demanded it, but she probably would not attend.

On New Year's Day 1940, Gladys Mary Baldwin walked down the aisle in Mansfield College Chapel in Oxford and believed happily she was going to share her life with a young lecturer living permanently in the peaceful academic other-worldliness of Oxford. She said that to be married to an Oxford don was her very idea of heaven.

But Harold Wilson was a man who had demonstrated early in his life that good things came in separate packages. Everything worked better for Harold if the different elements of his life – family, work, politics – were kept separate.

Sir William Beveridge – the economist, Liberal politician and social reformer at University College – took on Harold Wilson as a researcher. Harold was diligent and worked long hours. At the weekends he often went to work at Beveridge's home in Avebury. Avebury was out of bounds for Mary. 'That part of his life, like his politics, belonged in a separate compartment,' observed Ben Pimlott. The Beveridge Report came out in 1942 and formed the basis for the social reforms brought in by the Labour government in 1945.

Harold became a civil servant during the war and the Wilsons moved to London and a series of rented flats. Mary was delighted to move back to Oxford when the war ended, but she was without her husband most of the time. Harold Wilson became MP for Ormskirk in the 1945 election and spent most of the next couple of years working frantically as a government minister. Mary and baby Robin stayed in Oxford, living in rooms at University College and pegging out the washing in the fellows' garden. Harold visited them at the weekends when he could, but that wasn't very often.

5

Marcia at Queen Mary

In autumn 2022, I went to visit Queen Mary, the university in east London where in 1954 Marcia was awarded a Bachelor of Arts degree in history. Queen Mary, in Marcia's day a college of the University of London, is now a standalone university and one of the prestigious twenty-four UK universities which form the Russell Group. Halfway between Stepney Green and Mile End Tube stations, it's surprising to find a campus university made up of red-brick accommodation blocks as well as lecture rooms, laboratories and libraries.

In a space the size of an inner-city school playground between the brick buildings, there's a simple dramatic and moving memorial.

The Novo is an old and now disused Jewish cemetery right in the heart of the university. It is roughly a quarter of the original burial ground opened in 1733 for the Sephardi Jews who had arrived in the capital in the 1650s, encouraged to settle here by Oliver Cromwell, who saw the economic advantage of having such a prosperous group of people in the City doing trade and business. Novo reached capacity in 1936 and was then abandoned.

In 1972, Queen Mary College acquired the site and slowly built around it piece by piece, the burials being exhumed to Brentwood in

Essex. The tombs are now low-level headstones laid flat and cover-
ing the whole area, representing how in the Jewish faith everyone in
death is equal. It's an incredibly impressive site, causing new arrivals
to stop in their tracks to try to find out more. Here on a windy autumn
day you can stand on a floating bridge across the memorials and the
East End's history feels very close. For so much of her working life,
Marcia was supported and close friends with men and women who
had made it from occupied Europe to Britain with little more than
the clothes they stood up in. They made new and successful lives in
Britain and gave generously to support Harold's governments and,
often enough, Marcia personally, when her life became very difficult.
Somehow, I think Marcia would be highly impressed by the work
her college had done to preserve this cemetery.

She registered at Queen Mary College in October 1951. She had
her higher school certificate with 'distinction' in English, a 'good' in
history and a 'pass' in geography from Northampton High School,
which she attended from 1943 to 1951. As was necessary in the 1950s,
she had stayed at school for a further year in the upper sixth and
studied Latin and conversational French. Latin was an essential
entry requirement for anyone doing an arts degree back then.

Marcia's husband-to-be George Edmund Charles Williams (Ed),
who had attended King Edward VI Grammar School in Essex, was
registered with a 'good' in advanced pure and applied maths, phys-
ics, geography and English. He had left school and attended Northampton Engineering College in 1950, which suggests an intriguing
possibility that he and Marcia may have met before they went on to
Queen Mary.

When Ed left university, he was not liable for National Service
so went to work for the de Havilland Aircraft company in Hatfield,

from where he moved to Boeing in Seattle, where he remained for the rest of his life. When he died in Seattle in 2022, he had been married to his second wife for forty years. They had several children and many grandchildren.

Margarete, Marcia's sister-in-law, remembered that Marcia and Ed had stayed friends all their lives and that he had visited Britain quite often and met up with Marcia to swap stories.

When Marcia and Ed arrived at Queen Mary in 1951, the college was a school of the University of London which taught arts, science and engineering. There were 900 students, of whom 100 were post-graduates. Queen Mary had been given its Royal Charter in 1934 because Mary of Teck was the Queen Consort to King George V.

Most of what happened to Marcia and Ed at Queen Mary goes unrecorded, but Marcia was for some of her time the secretary of the student Labour Society.

On 14 May 1954, *The Cub*, the university's student newspaper, carried two pieces by Marcia – probably her only political writing under her own name until she left the government in 1976 and had a column in the *Mail on Sunday*. The first reported a visit by the local MP:

It was a rare pleasure to hear an MP speaking with such sincerity as Mr Sorensen displayed when addressing the Lab Soc for their first meeting this term at the Hatton on 30 April.

He had chosen a most difficult subject, 'Christianity and Socialism', and treated it more from the point of view of personal beliefs than hard facts or a strictly party line.

Mr Sorensen started by giving us his definitions of Christianity and socialism, which we saw were very similar, the first being

approximately 'love thy neighbour' and the second 'love thy enemies and competitors'. He also equated the Christian view of the
Kingdom of Heaven with the socialist ideal of a Brave New World.
By showing us these parallels between Christian and socialist
ideals, he did much to persuade us of the validity of his argument
that Christianity applied to modern life produces socialism.

In dealing with questions, Mr Sorensen was particularly impressive for contrary to the vast majority of public speakers, he
dealt firmly with the subject raised and attempted an answer.
This was seen for instance when Mr Sorensen was asked about
co-ownership. He gave his opinion it might be a valuable exper-
iment in small industries but was impractical for large ones like
steel and coal.

People who came to the meeting expecting a party haggle may
have been disappointed for what we heard was more an expres-
sion of convictions than an attempt to score party points, but no
one could fail to admire Mr Sorensen's sincerity or overlook the
impact of his character.

Marcia demonstrated clearly, right from this first report, that she
had a clear appreciation of what politics was all about. She was
quick to make a judgement that Sorensen spoke sense and spoke
fairly. Twenty years later, she was to have dealings with him when
she was the Prime Minister's political secretary: offering him a seat
in the Lords to make a quick vacancy in Leyton for Patrick Gordon
Walker, who was appointed too speedily by Harold as his first Foreign Secretary but then lost his Smethwick seat to a racist candidate.
'If you want a nigger for a neighbour, vote Labour' was successfully whispered to the voters of Smethwick, and Gordon Walker

was defeated. Wilson wanted to keep Gordon Walker as Foreign Secretary so Sorensen resigned from Leyton. Gordon Walker stood and lost again. Sorensen accepted a peerage and then promptly proposed the abolition of the Lords in favour of a senate of experts in administration.

Marcia also demonstrated by a second report in *The Cub* that right from her beginning in student politics, she could be a harsh critic when she felt it necessary. A Dr Weyman gave a talk to Labour students on the H-bomb and got a dismissive response from Marcia:

> Dr Weyman gave his talk to an audience consisting perhaps significantly of 31 men and 2 women.
>
> His discourse upon the nature of the construction and the devastating effects of the H-bomb was interesting, lucid and doubtless accurate.
>
> The desirability of international control of the bomb needed little stressing and Dr Weyman very sensibly did not elaborate on the question.
>
> Unfortunately, the speaker's clear thinking did not extend to 'means and method'. His answers to a particularly poor set of questions were unrelated and sometimes contradictory.
>
> Whilst not doubting Dr Weyman's sincerity, one cannot help wondering if he had complete mastery of the subject.

In a couple of sentences, Marcia had written off Dr Weyman's chances of being asked to speak again to the Labour students at Queen Mary.

Here she was at just twenty-two, fearlessly expressing her judgement on the speaker. It was a talent she never lost.

Once she graduated from Queen Mary, Marcia continued her studies at St Godric's Secretarial College in Hampstead, learning shorthand and typing. She clearly excelled and within the year, she was a junior secretary at Transport House, the Labour Party's headquarters led by General Secretary Morgan Phillips. Her political career was finally beginning; Marcia the politician was on her way to Westminster.

6

The Post-War Labour Party

The 1945 general election produced a landslide victory for Labour. It was ten years since the last election, and during the war years, there had been a coalition government with Winston Churchill as Prime Minister and Clement Attlee as his deputy.

Labour had worked hard knocking at doors across the land to outline their progressive ideas and promise social reform. Those who had fought to win the war were promised they could now win the peace.

Harold Wilson was just twenty-nine years old and the new MP for Ormskirk. He was very well qualified. His work as a researcher for Sir William Beveridge at University College, Oxford, was on social reform, and when he had signed up to serve at the start of the war he had been sent to London as a civil servant. By 1945, he had gained a reputation for prodigious energy and mental agility. Most people who become MPs, however promising, must do time as a backbencher, but Harold was given a ministerial job immediately as parliamentary secretary at the Ministry of Works. He worked ferociously hard, often sixteen hours a day. His wife and child, Mary and Robin, continued to live in rooms in University College in Oxford and Harold visited at weekends when he could, which wasn't often.

Mary complained that one long summer he had managed only two weekends with his family. The compartmentalisation of Harold's life was there for all to see. Work was and always would be his first concern. Harold was promoted to Secretary for Overseas Trade and was away in the USA for three months leading a delegation to the Food and Agriculture Organization.

Andrew Roth, an American journalist who settled in Britain in the 1950s, made a considerable contribution to the study of British politics. His *Parliamentary Profiles* and *Westminster Confidential* newsletter were widely read by journalists and foreign embassies eager for British gossip. Just a year after Harold Wilson retired, Roth brought out a biography: *Sir Harold Wilson: Yorkshire Walter Mitty*. The title suggested that Wilson was a meek and mild fantasist and a dreamer like Thurber's Mitty. It didn't really fit Wilson, a planner and an organiser who kept his life neatly filed in separate compartments and tried hard to improve future chances for the Labour Party, but it stuck.

One chapter in the book, 'A man with two wives', caused serious trouble: 'While at the peak of his political prowess, Harold Wilson lived atop a "landmine" of tremendously destructive potential. Its explosive force derived from his triangular relationship with two women, one repelled, the other fascinated by politics.'

Mary Wilson was identified as the wife at home and Marcia Williams as the wife in the office. Both Roth and Joe Haines in 1977 ranted about Harold's political dependence on Marcia and her ability to humiliate him in front of colleagues, but Roth also brought up the intriguing possibility of a relationship between Mary and another man.

Roth claimed that Mary Wilson had met another man while her

husband was in the USA working with the Food and Agriculture Organization.

Roth referred to her *Selected Poems*, published twenty-four years later.

Mary had included a poem about a meeting with a man on a crowded train. The unknown man had picked the moment to explain to Mary that they must end their relationship. She wondered if he had picked the train so that she would not be able to make a fuss. She demonstrated how personal the poem was by using her name in the verse: 'Mary,' said the suitor, 'We must never meet again.'

Well, who knows? Perhaps Mary's poem was a dramatic piece of fiction designed to attract Harold's attention. He was already well known for his stern habit of compartmentalising his life. Work always came first in the life of the non-conformist Yorkshire politician. Did Mary write her poems to try to win back a wandering husband whose first passion would always be politics? The Wilsons sued and the early editions of Andrew Roth's book were withdrawn, but as with so many libel actions back then, money was exchanged, and the case forgotten. Today you can find the long-forgotten *Sir Harold Wilson: Yorkshire Walter Mitty* with its story about Mary and her mysterious love for a few pounds in second-hand bookshops.

To check the verse itself, I bought an autographed first edition of Mary Wilson's bestselling poems for £3 and found Roth hadn't been totally accurate. He had taken some lines from two separate poems and combined them to make his case that bit more compelling, but he certainly came up with a plausible explanation of the way the Wilsons were to go on to run their marriage.

Roth claims that when Harold returned from the USA for Christmas 1946, Mary confessed what had happened. There's no reason given as to why she confessed. Maybe she invented a confession as the end to an invented love affair? Whatever the truth of the matter, Harold took it calmly, as he did all things to do with Mary or Marcia. Mary was upset, mightily furious that he was not furious. She said he simply made it clear that he wanted them to stay together and that he wanted appearances to be maintained. Harold stressed it was important that the then Prime Minister Clement Attlee and his wife should not find out. Roth says Mary was angry that Harold could put his political career first, livid that he remained so calm in the face of the devastating news she had delivered.

Harold's reaction was important, and a convincing pointer to the way he always was to behave with Marcia throughout their life together. There could be terrible scenes from Marcia, she could rant and rave, and he would sigh and get on with his work. When a civil servant complained to the Prime Minister that he had put up with four years of Marcia's intemperate behaviour, Harold merely nodded and said, 'I've put up with fourteen.'

But according to Roth, Harold set about repairing the situation with Mary. If what he says is correct, it suggests an early agreement between Mary and Harold about the way their future would be conducted. Politics would play no part in their home life together. What happened in Westminster would stay in Westminster.

Harold, if he thought about it at all, would probably have realised that he needed help and support on two separate fronts. A wife at home to run the family and a knowledgeable and dedicated partner in the office. Barbara Pym's novel *No Fond Return of Love*, published in 1961, is all about the contribution women were expected to make to marriages and working partnerships. Men were clearly labelled the boss and the breadwinner; in return for this package, women at home must mastermind the household and bring up the children, and in the office they must work diligently for long hours organising and assisting their men to success. Viola Dace in *No Fond Return of Love* gives her time for free to write a detailed index for academic Dr Aylwin Forbes's latest book, but without regard for her contribution (he had never seen her as any more than a dull middle-aged frump), she was unceremoniously dumped, for a curvaceous teenager. In 1961, Barbara Pym's men needed and expected lots of support from the women in their lives, and so did Harold Wilson.

Andrew Roth tells us that when Harold returned to Washington in the New Year, he took Mary with him, and Robin was left with his grandparents in Richmond. Mr and Mrs Wilson had three weeks together in Washington and returned to Britain on the *Queen Elizabeth* at the end of January 1947.

Later that year, Harold was made president of the Board of Trade and joined the Cabinet. Mary found she was pregnant with their second child. With a ministerial salary of £500 and a loan from Herbert, Harold's dad, the young Wilsons were able to afford the deposit and repayments on a mortgage of £5,000 on No. 10 Southway, Hampstead Garden Suburb.

Mary seemed happy with their new home in north London, but she was ruthless in keeping politics and politicians well away from family life. Very few people were invited to visit the Wilsons at home, but that was very much the way of things in post-war Britain. The only guests in many homes were visiting relatives. Robin Wilson came home from school one day and said to his mother, 'People are saying Dad is important. Is this true?'

'All dads are important,' explained Mary.

Inside the Labour Party, people were divided about Harold.

There was agreement that he was clever and hard-working, but how to answer the age-old Labour question, where did he stand in the party, was he left or right? No one was quite sure, but he was certainly dubbed unfashionable. They knew he had studied at Oxford, but he was seen by many insiders as provincial and unpretentious. A clever grammar schoolboy from the north who loved fish and chips with bread and butter and a generous souse of malt vinegar accompanied by a pot of Yorkshire tea.

Just 2.4 miles south of the Garden Suburb en route to the House of Commons is Frognal, the smartest part of Hampstead. Large old red-brick villas with generous gardens climb the hill between Finchley Road and Hampstead High Street. In the 1940s and '50s, Labour's Leader of the Opposition Hugh Gaitskell lived at 18 Frognal Gardens. In 2023's money, it would cost between £7 million and £8 million to buy one of the houses there.

Gaitskell and his wife Dora held endless salons and soirées for their followers in theatre and the arts, who, along with enlightened academics, Euro-enthusiasts and sympathetic businessmen, swirled enthusiastically around Her Majesty's Leader of the Opposition and his shadow Cabinet. They began as Gaitskellites and were refined to the even more exclusive Frognalites as they were awarded invitations to the Labour leader's exclusive gatherings at home.

Gaitskell was in his fifties and enjoyed the company of friends and colleagues who had been with him at Oxford. Sophisticated arts lovers who mostly sent their children to expensive private schools and spent their holidays in France and Italy, or in country houses at home.

Harold Wilson distrusted the Frognalites, particularly Anthony Crosland and his friends. He saw them as an upper-middle-class clique of Oxford pals. Crosland similarly disliked Wilson and in private referred to him as 'dirty little Wilson'. This mutual dislike based on class was clearly evident. Journalists who could see what the Frognalites thought of Wilson rumoured that he and Mary had 'ducks on the wall' of their front room in Hampstead Garden Suburb. Note for youthful readers: in 1938, Beswick Pottery produced china mallard ducks in five sizes, and it became fashionable after the war for the aspirational lower middle classes to have a set flying across their sitting room wall. Today, a perfect set are seen as quirky 'mid-century' gems and cost from £300 to £500 per flight on eBay.

In the 1960s, many of the middle-class MPs in the Labour Party lived in London and visited their constituencies infrequently. When my family, the Mitchells, landed homeless in Grimsby in 1977 behind our brand-new MP Austin, we were told that Anthony Crosland, the previous member who had died suddenly and unexpectedly at the age of fifty-eight, had come to town just twice a month, calibrated with Grimsby Town's home matches. He attended a constituency advice surgery in the mornings, had lunch with the football club directors, watched the match and was back in London or his country home near Banbury in time for dinner. My husband immediately announced, Wilson style, without consulting me, that we were all coming to live in Grimsby as soon as possible. Being a producer/director on World in Action at Granada Television in Manchester, just a forty-minute train journey from our home in Sowerby Bridge, I was speechless. Like most young women then, I couldn't drive. Grimsby by public transport meant two changes at Leeds and Doncaster and it could take more than three hours to get there. Like Mary Wilson, I was furious that his work was top

of the agenda. I was lucky enough to find a similar job at Thames
Television in London. Still three hours from Grimsby, but at least in
those days it was on a direct train line, and we needed a place to stay
there if Austin was to represent the interests of his new constituents.
Looking back after years of holding it against him, I understand
now that he saw the Crosland approach as hopelessly old fashioned
and well... conservative. It would be impossible to imagine the
Frognalites running the Labour Party today when voters don't just
expect MPs to live in the constituency – they prefer them to have
been born there as well.

Gaitskell, who was popular as well as opinionated, had soundly
defeated left-winger Aneurin Bevan for the leadership, and when
the 1960s arrived, Labour seemed to be well on their way to winning the next general election while being firmly led from the right
of centre.

But Gaitskell suddenly became ill with lupus: an incurable illness
where the body's immune system mistakenly attacks healthy parts
of the body. These days symptoms can often be treated with med-
icines that reduce inflammation. Back in the 1960s, drugs were
less sophisticated and death rates were higher. Medical staff at the
Middlesex Hospital fought hard to save him, but Hugh Gaitskell
died on 18 January 1963; he was just fifty-six. As Chancellor of the
Exchequer, Gaitskell had been firmly to the right of centre and to
pay for rearmament had introduced the first deeply unpopular cuts
to the NHS budget. Spectacles and false teeth were to be removed
from the NHS's free list and would need to be paid for separately by
patients. There was an exemption for children, the poor and the ill.
The situation still holds today, but back then it was a move fiercely

opposed by the man Gaitskell defeated for the leadership, left-winger Aneurin Bevan.

During his time as Labour leader, Gaitskell had tried to modernise the party by ditching a famous part of its constitution, Clause IV, which promised that under a Labour government the means of production – in other words the makers in factories, mines, power stations and the like – should be owned by the state, but his proposal was rejected by Labour Party members and Clause IV lasted thirty-four more years until Tony Blair succeeded in changing the constitution of the party in 1997.

Just two months before Gaitskell's death, shadow Foreign Secretary George Brown, he of the sharp and intrusive questions to Khrushchev's son in the Harcourt Room on the night when Harold and Marcia first met, had soundly defeated Harold Wilson in a contest to become Gaitskell's deputy. Harold appeared a lonely figure in the party, isolated and unsupported in a profession where supporters are key to upwards progression. Enter Marcia Matilda Williams, aged twenty-four, a year out of Queen Mary College, London, under a year married to Ed Williams – a 23-year-old, card-carrying Conservative aerospace engineer also from Queen Mary.

7

Marcia and Harold: A Growing Partnership

Inside the Labour Party, Harold Wilson was seen as surefooted but from the left. Yes, he had been to Oxford, but he was an Oxford-educated man with a Yorkshire accent and regional tastes. He wasn't a polished pro-European. He didn't court a group of MPs and entertain them at home. In fact, he didn't have a group of MPs around him at all. He and Mary and their two sons lived quietly at 10 Southway, Hampstead Garden Suburb. 'The Suburb', a twentieth-century addition to north London, was the idea of Henrietta Barnett, a Christian socialist who had witnessed the housing conditions of the poor in her husband's inner London parish. The Suburb was designed to cater for families of all incomes and all social classes, and the Wilsons loved it. It was a few minutes' drive and a whole world away from the Gaitskells' Victorian red-brick villa in Frognal. Just like Tony Crosland who represented Grimsby and many of the distinctly middle-class Labour MPs, Harold never made a home in his Merseyside constituency. Unlike Crosland and the Gaitskellites, however, Harold had popular tastes and all their lives he and Mary enjoyed living modestly among ordinary folks. Harold enjoyed sing-songs round the piano, D'Oyly Carte opera, fish and chips with malt vinegar and cold pork pies and HP sauce. He was very close to his parents and sister and proud of his home life, Mary and their two boys, but politics played no part in any of that. From the beginning, Harold compartmentalised his life, and that never changed. At work, he watched where he put his feet, but he walked alone among Labour politicians. When they got together in 1956, Marcia immediately understood that, and quickly became his closest political ally in every way and remained that for the rest of their lives. She eagerly took the job he offered her as his secretary, but from the beginning she was so much more. 'By the end of her first year, she had become his early warning system,' said Ben Pimlott.

Until he became chairman of the Public Accounts Committee, a job he combined with his role as shadow Chancellor, and moved to the Commons, Harold and Marcia worked together every morning in the boardroom at Montague L. Meyer. He picked her up from her north London home after he'd dropped his sons at school. She was his secretary, organiser, general factotum and gatekeeper, nearby but protected from the hullabaloo of the House of Commons.

In 1957, not long after Marcia started working with Harold, his mother Ethel died of cancer at her home in Cornwall with her husband Herbert and her children Marjorie and Harold by her side. The very special relationship between the Yorkshire mother and her life's project, her son Harold, was over. Harold was deeply hurt – he couldn't quite believe she had gone – but this was one of the gaps that Marcia did so much to fill.

Over the years, in their attempts to describe the relationship between Harold and Marcia, some observers said he treated her as an adored daughter and others could see that she in some ways replaced his mother when she criticised him as if he were a badly behaved child who had disappointed her.

But from the beginning of their working relationship, they appeared to share a very great deal, and those around them were fascinated.

Peter Shore, who was head of the Labour Party's research department and later became Prime Minister Wilson's first parliamentary private secretary, observed Harold and Marcia together: 'She pierced his complacency on many occasions. She disturbed him. Made him see things in a different way, more than anyone else I can recall.'

Harold and Marcia shared a modernising zeal, and a total belief in Harold Wilson. She became the controller of their situation early on. It's doubtful that he worried too much about her situation. Their relationship was based on his need for her; he could see she knew what she was doing for him, and he let her get on with it.

It was a unique relationship and it stood the test of time. Years later, before he began to resent Marcia's closeness to Harold, Joe Haines wrote:

She met for a great many years a deep craving within him: for someone else to whom politics was meat and drink and the very air that was breathed; someone who, at her best, had a political mind capable of testing and matching his; someone who, again at her best, possessed a deadly ability to slash her way through the woolliness and verbiage of political argument to get to the heart of an issue. Someone who was prepared to devote all her time to Harold Wilson's service; and someone who, at the very worst moments, was always there.

There was just six years between the death of Ethel Wilson and the election of her son Harold as the leader of the Labour Party. Marcia Williams cemented herself firmly in place and fought hard to make it happen.

Just before Christmas 1955, Marcia had married Ed Williams in the parish church in her home village of West Haddon in North-amptonshire. Around the time Marcia started working with Harold, Ed had left England and gone to work as an aerodynamic engineer for the Boeing Company in Seattle, USA. In the early days, Marcia visited him for holidays. They'd had a fluid agreement that soon he would come back to live in the UK, but it never quite happened. Marcia was worried about it and certainly had no plans to live in the USA. Marcia and Ed got on well enough, but they were two am-bitious people who were planning to travel in opposite directions in their careers, just as they had at university where he was chair of the Conservative students at Queen Mary and she ran the Labour Society. George Caunt wrote in his unpublished manuscript that Marcia had confessed to her friends at Transport House that she realised she'd made a big mistake very early in her married life with Ed. Their careers were destined to keep them apart.

Ed had seen Marcia's passion for politics and her naked ambition, but he had failed to spot an important change in her focus during the short time she had been working with Harold. She alone had di-agnosed Harold Wilson's political possibilities with confidence, and as far as she was concerned, he was the future of the Labour Party. The vital clue was that in those early days it was Marcia who was convinced that Harold could make it to 10 Downing Street. He was much more diffident, he knew he was isolated by the right-wingers, he felt they distrusted him, and it was the same with the officials at head office. But Marcia was a lioness. If it was 'Wilson against the world' – and with her youthful and rebellious spirit she believed it was – then she was staying with him in Britain to protect him and guide him, and Ed Williams was already too late to save their marriage.

Regularly, Marcia wrote to ask her husband when he would come back to England. He was never quite sure. Eventually, a letter arrived to say that he had decided to stay in Seattle for good. He had met a girl at a Christmas party and fallen in love with her and he wanted a divorce. In January 1960, Harold and Marcia made a trip to the USA. Harold went on to China; Marcia went on to Seattle. Harold was on a speaking tour, earning money to pay the salaries of his staff and the office expenses. When he finished his work, he joined Marcia in Seattle. Together they spoke to Ed and agreed a deal. Just over a year later, Ed Williams was granted a decree nisi in King County, Washington state, on 7 April 1961. Marcia, who was discreet about everything until the day she died, kept her divorce secret from the people she worked with in London. Her marriage had ended two years before the death of Gaitskell.

The Labour Party of the late 1950s was deeply split. Gaitskell and his followers were mostly Oxford and Cambridge graduates who had been friends at university and sometimes even at school before that. They were often from rich families and loved and patronised the arts, music and literature. Harold Wilson and those on the left tended to be social reformers who wanted to remove class barriers. Harold was seen as dry and dull by many of his colleagues, but with Marcia watching over him and coaching him furiously, Harold's performances in the House of Commons began to improve. He began to take a lighter and sharper tone in his speeches. Chancellor

Harold Macmillan and Harold Wilson began to enjoy jousting with one another at the dispatch box. MPs started gathering to listen to their arguments. Gaitskell was pleased that his shadow Chancellor had become such a success, but according to Roy Jenkins, Gaitskell still saw Wilson as 'a tricky fellow'. Wilson made a challenge to Gaitskell's leadership in 1960 and tried to take over the deputy leadership from George Brown in 1962. Both attempts failed and Wilson enhanced his reputation for divisiveness and disloyalty.

In December 1962, Hugh Gaitskell fell ill with flu, but his doctor declared him well enough to travel to the Soviet Union, where he met Nikita Khrushchev for talks.

In January 1963, Harold was back in the USA again when Gaitskell took a turn for the worse. Marcia was working in their large office in the House of Commons allocated to the chairman of the Public Accounts Committee, one of Harold's new roles. The windows looked out onto the icy terrace and the grey River Thames. Marcia phoned Harold with daily progress reports. She warned that things had become very serious with the leader's health but counselled it could look opportunistic if Harold cancelled his programme and hastened home.

Hugh Gaitskell died in the Middlesex Hospital on 18 January 1963, and Harold was back in the UK by the next morning. The race for the Labour leadership was on, with George Brown taking on the role in the interim.

In 1963, the choosing of a new leader was simple. Only Labour MPs took part in the ballot. Wilson had alienated the right when he had tried to beat Gaitskell out of a job in 1960 and George Brown in 1962, and the left seemed doubtful and a bit confused.

Then someone appeared who claimed he could win the election

for Harold: ex-military colonel and conspiracy theorist George Wigg, the MP for Dudley, another new arrival at the 1945 election. Wigg wasn't a popular man at Westminster. He loved gossip and always had a tale to tell. He was passionately interested in security matters and was willing to take a bet on almost anything. Wigg was a Londoner, from Ealing where his dad had been a milkman and a hopeless alcoholic who drowned in a local lake. 'Death by misadventure' ruled the coroner. Wigg's mum had to bring up six children on her own. George was the eldest and he'd worked at his father's side from his tenth birthday. He joined the army when he left school and rose quickly through the ranks during the war to be a colonel in the Army Educational Corps. He had been planning to emigrate to Canada when the war ended, but his enthusiasm for politics led him to run and be elected as the MP for Dudley in 1945, when his turbulent career as a politician began. Despite other MPs failing to warm to him, Wigg quickly mastered the procedure of the House of Commons and began using it to his advantage. It was Wigg who later in his career managed to draw attention in the House to the sex life and scandal surrounding the War Minister John Profumo who had an affair with model Christine Keeler at a time when she was also involved with a spy from the Russian embassy. Wigg ultimately brought about Profumo's downfall when he managed to introduce Profumo's friendship with Keeler in a speech in the Commons. He also played an important part in the prosecution of a suspected serial killer, John Bodkin Adams, by exposing, again in the House, the procedural weaknesses in the case put forward by the Attorney General Reginald Manningham-Buller.

Wigg was known as an emotional man prone to hero worship. He attached himself passionately to those he followed, and Harold

Wilson became his latest obsession. Wigg was impatient, intolerant, quick tempered and merciless to those he regarded as incompetent and ineffective, but like Wilson he was loyal to his friends. He had a zeal for helping those who he felt had been badly treated and he could be both charming and devastatingly rude.

Wigg liked and supported Wilson, and Wilson trusted him. He enjoyed hearing Wigg's gossip and listened eagerly when Wigg put forward plans to make Wilson the next Labour leader. Wilson and Wigg shared a strong interest in the security services, and Wilson came to rely on Wigg to let him know what was going on behind the scenes. Wigg's offer to run Wilson's campaign to become leader of the Labour Party was happily accepted.

The campaign relied on gossip and innuendo and benefited from Wigg's lifelong passion for gambling. He went around the tea rooms in the Commons asking for the odds on his bet that Wilson would be the next leader. 'I want to back Wilson, how much will you lay?' he asked the MP for Caerphilly, trade unionist Ness Edwards. Edwards hesitated and Wigg said boldly, 'Fifty pounds?' Edwards replied, 'Two pounds.'

Wigg writes in his autobiography: 'I closed the deal with a comment. You can't hold your views very strongly, but I'll take it.'

Word quickly went round that Wigg was prepared to back Wilson for £50. By the end of the evening, the figure had gone up to £100, and, to Wiggs's delight, two days later, gossips were reporting it as £500.

Wigg was also to note in his memoir:

This was the first occasion on which I took notice of Mrs Marcia Williams, for some years Wilson's secretary. My impression was of a competent, hard-working shorthand typist. Since she possessed a university degree, she was obviously well qualified to act as secretary to a busy politician who was about to become Leader of the Labour Party and soon to be Prime Minister.

Of course, Marcia made a much bigger contribution than Wigg or anyone else realised. Roy Jenkins believed she was the most talented politician in Wilson's circle. She kept everything under control. She advised Wilson wisely and he listened to her.

Harold Wilson won the Labour Party leadership election in February 1963. Marcia explained to Austin Mitchell that Harold was elected as a left-of-centre candidate:

Gaitskell was much loved by the party machine, so the Establishment of the Labour Party as with the majority of the Parliamentary Labour Party, were right of centre, governed in the main by trade unions and trade union money, and when Harold came in as leader it came as a great shock to them that they had got a left-of-centre leader. I don't think Harold ever gained love and affection from, say, party headquarters. Respect is one thing. They respected him because he was the winner, and he was also efficient and knew how to operate the system. He had worked out how to beat the Tories at their own game and that was the real reason why he was the winner.

Everyone thinks that there was masses of time between Harold becoming the leader of his party and taking them into an election, but it was a very short period. It was sixteen months, and the '63 leadership election campaign was a very vicious campaign from which the party in my view never recovered. The right wing indulged in practices which were not really acceptable and used Tories to help them do it, and that sort of poison stayed. Harold never thought of himself as embattled because he was a technocrat, really. I suppose you could say he believed in getting on with what had to be done and he knew the means by which he was going to do it and he was immensely interested in the mechanics of it all. He could actually lose himself in those mechanics. He loved to work out what the headline was going to be in the newspaper the next day and he had a gift for working out his press release for each speech because it would have a soundbite that would absolutely dominate the next day's headlines.

But Barbara Castle believed the right wing from the beginning had far too much influence.

They were plotting against Harold all the time. They hated his guts. He had succeeded their beloved Gaitskell. That was an unforgiveable sin. Mind you they knew perfectly well that George Brown would have been disastrous and the Parliamentary Labour Party (PLP) rejected the idea of Jim Callaghan. They thought he was too lightweight. Harold, who had been working for this all the way along, very skilfully almost got it by default. And the very first thing he did in that PLP meeting when he beat George Brown for the leadership was to say, 'I do hope George will be my deputy.' He knew he was taking a snake to his bosom but that was what he did. George's only reply was to stalk off the platform and sulk. Eventually his own right wing persuaded him not to be a fool.

When Harold became Leader of the Opposition, there was a

photograph published in a London newspaper of Harold and Mary's tea party with Marcia and an unknown man, described as Marcia's husband Ed. George Caunt says that, given the timing, the 'husband' in the photograph was actually Marcia's geologist brother, Tony Field.

Marcia and Harold, together and isolated from the mainstream of the party, had a really tough time preparing for the 1964 election. Marcia recalled:

Everything we did from beginning to end was done on a shoe-string because it was done in the days before public funding. There was nothing for a leader of the party. If he wanted to run a campaign – which Harold knew he had to do if he wanted to win – you had to have two campaigns, one that runs from party headquarters and one that you run yourself. You couldn't do it unless you were skilful or had loads of money. But we had passion and belief and absolute determination that we were going to win. We had excitement. We worked hours that when I think about it now were beyond credibility.

He was a one-man band and he just had me in the office, to run the office. I did his publicity and his press relations. If anyone rang up from the newspapers, I took those calls and gave the messages back. We had half a secretary who also worked for George Brown. She was provided by Transport House, and we had a girl clerk who could do all the daily fetching and carrying.

All the rest was done by himself and yours truly helping out. That's it. There was nothing else and no money.

Marcia and Harold fighting the 1964 election for Labour were as

successful a double act as their musical contemporaries Lennon and
McCartney. They were also both equally eager to learn lessons from
their frequent visits to the USA observing the way the Democrats
fought elections. They saw themselves as young and modern and
interdependent.

Marcia remembered:

There were resemblances, great resemblances between the way
the economies of America and Britain were. Both of them had
slowed down and both of them had got out of date and industry
was badly managed. Their Kennedy campaign was to get America
moving again and we used it blatantly – we took it – and our PR
team came up with 'Get Britain going again'. It was a good slogan
because it described how everything had come to a standstill and
you needed to get some life back into the system. So we watched
how that had been done. Harold knew a lot of the Kennedy
people; he had taught some of them at Oxford. He knew a lot of
the Kennedy White House too, so we did get a lot of ideas from
them, but you can't actually translate America to Britain as it's not
really possible to fight Blackburn and Bolton and Newcastle and
Truro in the way that you would fight Chicago.

An important reason why that couldn't happen was that British
Labour politicians didn't have wealthy backers like their American
colleagues. Harold and Marcia badly needed financial supporters in
order to win the 1964 general election. Enter Joseph Kagan and his
wife Margaret (previously Margarita Shtromaite).

One day in the late '50s on a train from London to Huddersfield, Joe Kagan introduced himself to a person he recognised from

pictures in the local paper: Huddersfield-born MP for Huyton Harold Wilson, who was opposition trade spokesman.

Joe Kagan was born Juozapas Kaganas in Kaunas, Lithuania, on 6 June 1915. His parents were Orthodox Jews, who had made a fortune in textiles by selling grey cloth for uniforms to the kaiser's army during the early years of the First World War. Joe received a technical education at Kaunas High School and at a German boarding school in East Prussia. He was keen to train as a barrister, but his father persuaded him to study textiles in England. He travelled to West Yorkshire, chaperoned by his mother, and gained a Bachelor of Commerce degree in textiles at Leeds University.

Joe then went home to run the family textile business but was stranded in Lithuania with his mother when the Russians invaded the independent Baltic republic in 1940. He was allowed to remain manager of the family firm by the Soviet authorities. This was an unusual concession and made people suspicious that he was being groomed to become a KGB agent. In June 1941, when the Nazi forces invaded Lithuania, he was stripped of his belongings and forced into a ghetto with his mother. On 23 October 1943, he married nineteen-year-old Margarita Shtromaite, the daughter of a middle-class Lithuanian family, at a makeshift registry office in the ghetto. It was only after the war that the couple formally exchanged rings at a Jewish ceremony in Bradford in 1946. Joe escaped ethnic cleansing and became a foundry worker, and when the ghetto became a concentration camp, he planned an ingenious escape by constructing a secret hideout in a container in the foundry roof, where he hid with his wife and her mother for nine months until Russian troops liberated Kaunas. The Kagans then travelled across Europe with other refugees to Romania, where Joe got a job for a year in the British mission at Bucharest as a pest-control officer. Then Joe and Margaret made their way to Elland in Calderdale, West Yorkshire, where Joe's dad had set up a small branch of the family textile company.

After working as a salesman for his father's business, Joe tried his hand in the motor trade before starting out on his own account in textiles with his wife Margaret, manufacturing rough blankets in a hastily erected shed with a corrugated iron roof at South End, Elland. It's still there today, part of an industrial estate where talented grafters work in freezing conditions in the Pennine winters to start tiny local businesses. I spent some time there in the winter of 2022. A brilliant local sculptor chipped away for months carving my husband's gravestone. Not for the first time I marvelled at how tough and determined Joe and Margaret had been. In 1951, Joe acquired the century-old firm of J. T. and T. Taylor of Batley, a pioneering profit-sharing company, and produced his first raincoat made of a waterproof unattractive knobbly nylon between green and khaki. There was an inner layer of a woven tartan wool. The two layers were firmly bonded together. The insulated material, which was light, waterproof and warm if deeply unlovely (to me anyway), was called Gannex and it was an instant hit.

When Joe Kagan introduced himself to the opposition trade spokesman Harold Wilson on the train between London and Huddersfield, they got on immediately. Harold Wilson wore his first Gannex coat on a world tour in 1956 and went on faithfully and proudly promoting them until they were taken up by world leaders across the globe, including US President Lyndon B. Johnson and Nikita Khrushchev, whom Wilson presented with a coat in 1963. Gannexes turned out to be a hit at home too. The Queen and the Duke of Edinburgh were often filmed wearing them at sporting events, and even the royal corgis had mini Gannexes for the cold weather. Arctic and Antarctic explorers, Himalayan climbers, the armed services and police forces in Britain and Canada were all wrapped up in Gannex outerwear. The success of the new fabric made Joe a multi-millionaire and put Kagan Textiles in control of one of the most efficient combines in the textile and clothing industries.

It wasn't too hard if you lived and worked in the 'northern media land' as I did in the 1960s to meet Joe Kagan. In fact, it was difficult to miss him as a Labour-supporting millionaire, a friend of Harold Wilson and a millowner in Elland and Todmorden famous for having invented the Gannex mac. Our house at Sowerby was less than ten minutes from Joe's place in Barkisland. My husband Austin Mitchell, then a local TV star of *Calendar*, Yorkshire television's early evening magazine programme, loved his Gannex. It was hard to stop him wearing it. He also loved listening to Joe's stories and got his first ever mention in *Private Eye* as the twelfth man in Joe Kagan's team of supporters of Harold Wilson.

Barry Cockcroft, a Yorkshire Television producer and a great mate of Austin's, persuaded Joe to sponsor the world knurr and spell championships, the revival of an ancient Yorkshire game which involved springing a small clay ball out of a trap and belting it hard, and as far as you could.

On the day of the world championships, a big Yorkshire crowd gathered on the moors behind the Spring Rock Inn in Elland with as many celebrities as YTV could muster. Fred Trueman, Geoffrey Boycott and all of Yorkshire's presenters, reporters and film crews including Austin, me and our tiny twins in their double pushchair were there on a Saturday outing.

There was a freezing moorland storm with everyone struggling to find the little clay balls in the bracken. It was a television disaster but our entrée into the Kagan circle which included all the bigwigs from the Halifax area, all of us brought together for parties, concerts and huge New Year's Eve parties at Barkisland Hall, the magnificent seventeenth-century wool merchant's house the Kagan family hosted their parties in. Joe was a generous host, ebullient and amiable but also a little mysterious. I found him ever ready to listen, shrewd in his evaluations of people and ready to talk about his own imprisonment and escape from the USSR, though less so about British politics and his friends, Harold Wilson and Marcia Williams. To me, at that stage a young mum and ambitious studio director of *Look North*, the local BBC programme in Manchester, the whole thing was impossibly glamorous. We were often invited for end of the week drinks on a Friday night. I would get the train from Manchester Victoria to Sowerby Bridge at the end of a long day at *Look North*, having run all the way from the studio in Piccadilly. Breathless, I usually spent the journey changing my clothes and putting on my makeup in one of the dark and evil-smelling British Rail toilets. When I hopped off the train and met Austin at Sowerby Bridge for the short journey up to the Kagans' house, I tried hard to look as though I had spent the day doing nothing much at all. Joe would be crouched over a small table playing chess. Huge cigar in his mouth, drink at his side. As a greeting, he would run his hand slowly down whichever part of you was nearest the chess board. But while Joe was famous for enjoying the company of women, he wasn't creepy – he was just like so many men at the time: best to keep an arm's length away. One famous Friday, the Kagans had acquired a microwave, an incredibly new and exciting toy. Joe showed us all the tricks it could perform, but the one he loved best was putting an unshelled fresh egg inside and counting how long it took to explode. It was quite a while before I found out that microwaves could do more useful tasks.

Disgruntled Tories regularly imputed that Joe Kagan was a Russian spy, an accusation which cut no ice in Yorkshire where he was a benefactor, saving jobs and enlivening the area. He was treated with sniffy suspicion generated to discredit Wilson in the Westminster bubble. He was generous to a fault. He supplied a building in the middle of town for the use of the Elland Labour Party. He helped Harold with his office costs at a time when MPs (even Leaders of the Opposition) were on tiny salaries and no expenses at all.

The Gannex mill factory was an early model of how modern factories ought to be. A nursery was provided for workers' children. Joe's own kids went there and Pauline, their nanny, was put in charge of it. But the person to whom Joe's help mattered most was Marcia Williams. When they first met, Marcia was a single woman living alone in central London and soon to be the right-hand woman in No. 10 Downing Street. When all that changed and her life became a secret world, it would be help from generous Joseph Kagan which saved her from total disaster.

But financial backing is not the only element that goes into winning a general election. Candidates must also present their vision for the future of Britain, in order to win the popular vote. On 1 October 1963, at the Labour Party conference in Scarborough, Harold Wilson gave a powerful address about the way Britain had to wake up and change and modernise:

The revolution cannot become a reality unless we are prepared to make far-reaching changes in economic and social attitudes which permeate our whole system of society. The Britain which is going to be forged in the white heat of this revolution will be no place for restrictive practices or outdated methods on either side of industry.

Wilson's 'white heat' speech became one of the most memorable political speeches given in the twentieth century and was fiercely emblematic of his desire to help Britain modernise. And as Marcia revealed, before he was Prime Minister, 'he never had a speechwriter'. She highlighted:

> He worked on the whole lot. He would take from the main speech the one or two pages that were given out as a press release and into those he would add the main points he wanted to cover in a catchy way, which is what they all do today. They were all written by hand in pen, and it was quite an achievement. He loved to sit with a board on his knee and the foolscap lined paper. He did it all by hand; he loved it. He loved writing ... So many words a day and then they would have been brought back to him having been typed up.

As his words make clear, Harold truly believed that the only way forward was to get Britain working again, turning to science and technology for a prosperous future. Harold said he wanted to replace the traditional cloth cap of the British worker with a white laboratory coat. He said later that he had been trying to find a new image for the Labour Party.

Thirty years later, Tony Blair managed that with 'New Labour', a red rose and a mantra of 'education, education, education'.

The political duo Harold Wilson and Marcia Williams triumphantly carried Labour to victory in the 1964 general election – the party's first win in thirteen years – but Labour entered Downing Street with a tiny majority. Just four seats.

For Marcia, the biggest test of all had arrived. In British history, there has only ever been room for one woman in Downing Street: the Prime Minister's wife.

8

Marcia and Harold in Downing Street

'It was one of the most exciting, exhilarating and exhausting elections I have ever been involved in. Everywhere there had been the same sense of something new happening. The "time for a change" mood enveloped everything,' reminisced Marcia in *Inside Number 10*.

The night of the 1964 election was a tense one indeed. Harold, Mary, the inner circle of the Kitchen Cabinet and other people from Labour headquarters were all extremely jumpy like Marcia herself. They went to bed very late in the Adelphi Hotel in Liverpool and got up after just a few hours to catch the London train from Lime Street Station.

Those were the days when the Adelphi, a marvellous listed building in Portland stone, just a few minutes' walk from the station, was incredibly glamorous. There were great halls with marble pillars and leather chairs grouped together among potted palms and tea tables and very important people talking business. I loved staying there and made frequent overnight visits to Liverpool when working for the BBC and then Granada Television in Manchester. There was a breathtaking mosaic swimming pool in the basement with gently dripping fountains and statues. Every time I sat drinking tea among the marble pillars, people would tell another tale of Harold Wilson and his supporters. The fact that a Prime Minister had won elections and come back to sleep at the Adelphi while the votes were being counted added to the glamour of a hotel whose earlier glory days had been the 1930s, when the guests would be the next day's passengers on trans-Atlantic liners headed for New York. In the 1960s, the Adelphi captured the spirit of Liverpool. The Prime Minister was an important symbol of success just like Bob Dylan, who was photographed on the hotel balcony waving to his adoring fans.

On the morning after the 1964 election, Harold Wilson, his wife, his right-hand woman Marcia and his team of close supporters stumbled forth to catch the early morning train to London. Harold and Mary shared a compartment and Marcia arranged for the blinds to be drawn so they could try to get some rest, but the train stopped at Crewe, Birmingham and Rugby and excited Labour supporters lined the platforms, waving and wishing them good luck. Harold and Mary waved back. As to the other members of the team, their only contact with the outside world during the journey was a battery-operated transistor radio which belonged to Tommy Balogh, soon to be the new Prime Minister's economic adviser. Through minutes of crackling static and long tunnels of silence, they became steadily gloomier as they believed they heard their majority melt away as they travelled south.

Euston Station was crowded with press and TV cameras and a sizeable throng of members of the public eager to catch a glimpse of the possible new Labour Prime Minister. The team travelled to Transport House on Smith Square and spent the next few hours nervously watching television. By mid-afternoon, it was clear that the tiny majority had held and Harold would indeed be Britain's next Prime Minister. Celebrations ensued.

A veritable crowd set out for Buckingham Palace. Mary and her sons Robin and Giles, Harold's dad and Marcia packed into two cars along with the Prime Minister elect and the regulation civil servants. They waited in the Equerry's Room while Harold had his audience with the Queen. 'As I remember it, the conversation centred on horses, though my knowledge of them is minimal and the Wilson family's less,' wrote Marcia. 'It struck me at the time as an ironic beginning to the white-hot technological revolution and the government that was to mastermind it.'

When Harold and Marcia arrived at No. 10 after the Labour election victory of 1964, they were a well-practised double act. They had established a way of working together which suited them both. They had kept themselves very much apart from the Labour Party head office crowd except when essential. They had talked endlessly and went on conversing long after everyone else had gone home. They had planned and plotted together. They knew one another very well indeed. Their sexual relationship, and it is difficult to believe it never happened, was long over.

When Harold won the leadership of the Labour Party, Harold and Marcia as a couple had moved on to something that seemed so much more important to both of them than what went on in their separate homes in north London. Together they had political ambition to transform Britain, to encourage people to feel they were free to make their own choices. To get Britain working again. They believed that Harold's passion, the 'white heat' of technology, would beat back the Tories and rid the country of their old-fashioned class-based attitudes. Growth was slow in Britain: Marcia's ex-husband Ed had gone to the USA to work as an aerodynamicist in a world-class company, Boeing, in Seattle, but Harold and Marcia believed he should have been able to do that in Britain.

What visionary couple, so satisfied to have found one another, who believed so determinedly in the power of their relationship to conquer all the political obstacles in their path, could give up the chance of such a bright future for Britain?

When Harold's mother died in 1957, Marcia seemed to have quickly taken over the part Ethel played in Harold's life. The role developed by the Yorkshire mothers whose aim was to be showered in glory when their brilliant sons scaled Everest, built the Sydney Opera House or became Prime Minister. Often as she became older and her life became more troubled and messy, Marcia would shout at Harold not like an abandoned lover – rather the disappointed mother who knew how much better he could behave if he really put his mind to it.

The solid, practical and affectionate partnership that Harold had with Mary was something they all had to manage between them. Harold knew Mary wanted a quiet suburban life with her husband and children. She didn't want to live in 10 Downing Street and said firmly she would have preferred to stay in Hampstead Garden Suburb. But that would never have worked without a public scandal. Their house in Southway was sold and, with quite a lot of supportive publicity, the Wilsons and their teenaged sons moved in to Downing Street. Harold had no need to sort the situation with Mary because there was no 'situation'. They had children to bring up, a family life to live. Harold, with his solid Yorkshire practicality and his skill at compartmentalising his life, didn't see a problem at all. He needed Mary and he needed Marcia in different ways. What could possibly be wrong with that? It made perfect sense to him and of course it was what the majority of adult women in the 1960s were expected to accept. The man of the family had a job, a career, a profession. Over a lifetime, he filled in a great many official forms, adding his name as 'head of the family' in answer to the first question. For hundreds of years, women had had to accept that theirs was a subservient role, and if they wanted to do something else then it would be an add-on. Men's wages far outstripped women's and were regarded as the key source of a family's income. Indeed, not all women went back to work after they married, with some employers like the foreign arm of the civil service banning married women from joining. If a woman won at Wimbledon, she got only a tiny percentage of what was paid to a male champion. When Tony Crosland died in 1977, I was stunned to see Susan Barnes, his wife, a distinguished American journalist, referred to as 'Mrs Crosland who writes in the newspapers under her pen-name Susan Barnes'. But times were beginning to change and both Mary Wilson and Marcia Williams had clear ideas of who they were and what they wanted to be.

Mary always struggled to escape politics for an ordinary life. She did her MP's wife duties grudgingly; all her life she was searching for the ordinary. Several communications between Mary and Marcia exist in Marcia's files in the Bodleian Library. Both women – with fountain pens, blue ink and small neat writing – wrote coolly to one another about the day-to-day running of a Prime Minister's life.

'Dear Mary, would you like to invite your own guests to the Trooping of the Colour, or shall I do it? Yours, Marcia.'

'Dear Marcia, I am happy for you to do it. Yours, Mary.'

Marcia was searching for something very different. She and

Harold were life partners in politics and their aim was to win elections and change Britain for the better, permanently.

As was custom and practice even in the '60s, a few weeks before the election, Sir Timothy Bligh, the principal private secretary to Sir Alec Douglas-Home and the most senior civil servant in No. 10, invited Marcia to visit him and to have a look at the set-up should Labour, as was looking possible from the opinion polls, win the election. Marcia was taken for a tour of the building and then at 4 p.m. precisely there was a visit to the private office where all the parliamentary private secretaries, the civil servants who run the Prime Minister's office and through that the government, gathered each day for tea.

'Not the sort of men', mused Marcia, 'that I envisaged as serving Harold.'

But those gentlemen in tailor-made dark suits sipping their tea from Crown Derby may well have been at university with the Labour ministers who came in with Harold. The trade unionists and manual workers that the Labour Party laid claim to as their own in the 1960s and '70s lived in a different world. It was part of Marcia's great strength that she could see the gulf between the middle class and the skilled workers so clearly, and worked hard to get rid of it.

Marcia said that Sir Timothy had made it very clear to her that there was no place for her, or her office colleagues, at No. 10. But, of course, he didn't mean Labour supporters; he meant bossy women.

When she reported his ideas to Harold, they agreed between them to disagree with Sir Timothy.

Marcia said, 'They knew I had been running Harold's private office in opposition. If he succeeded in capturing power in 1964, they wanted to make sure that they captured him.'

When Labour won with a tiny majority of four seats, Marcia realised immediately how difficult the situation was bound to be. On the day after the election, she sat alone in silence in Downing Street watching the removal men taking away the Maudling family's furniture from No. 11.

Thirty years later, she told Austin Mitchell how she felt:

You are walking into a monastery, in No. 10 terms. The moment you go through that door, the silence is the first thing that strikes you, almost as if there is nothing happening and there is no one there, and it's very intimidating. If you go into a religious house at least there is an air of godliness, an air of spirituality about it, but in there it is quite threatening, that silence, because you are not sure what is going on behind all the closed doors that you are walking past. And you quickly find out that it is not as happy and pleasant as you thought it would be. The campaign was so exciting. It was a crusade. We were going to get Britain moving again, we were going to change the face of Britain. We were going to get working men represented. Suddenly, you enter a door, and it shuts behind you and you can't just say, 'Help! Let me out!' You are there, and you make the best of a bad job, and you try to work out what you are going to do.

I regard myself as a pioneer. I had to trailblaze for them and I had to suffer an awful lot of indignity and insults on the way. Nevertheless, my political office is still there, it's still functioning, and nobody has said we don't need it. They kept it and I think it is one of the most valuable things that have happened in Downing Street.

As Marcia waited in Downing Street on the very first day of Harold's premiership, she thought about the complications which lay ahead.

Harold was hit immediately by the magnitude of it all. It was devastating for him. There he had been twenty-four hours before, campaigning on a policy of getting Britain moving again, putting enthusiasm into everyone's hearts, only to be presented on the Friday afternoon with those small pieces of paper civil servants carry around with them, and this time indicated the magnitude of the problems he had to deal with.

There seemed to Marcia that lonely afternoon to be a stark choice between devaluation, import quotas or import taxes and thinking the unthinkable, perhaps all three of them.

'We had this tiny majority and this enormous economic problem. How could a socialist government hope to carry out the policies to which it was committed with an economic problem of this size and a majority in Parliament that hardly existed?'

Over forty-five years later, George Osborne had a similar experience when he read the jokey note from Labour's then Chief Secretary to the Treasury, Liam Byrne, wishing him good luck and announcing that there was no money left. It turned out to be cruelly true and the beginning of the next period of austerity.

Marcia turned to her own problems. Her role was quite clear to her. She was Harold's political secretary. John Wyndham had done the same job for Harold Macmillan, and everyone seemed to have accepted that. But Wyndham was a man, a man with the right sort of background. He had been to Eton and Cambridge and was later to become Lord Egremont in Macmillan's retirement honours. And he had worked without pay. Marcia was a woman without money and with a dad who was a builder in Northamptonshire. Yes, she had a degree and a shorthand typing qualification, but the Labour Party had certainly not offered to pay her wages – Harold would have to do that. Marcia could see the difference.

Today, all leading politicians have spads (special advisers). There are hundreds of them all over Whitehall. You will understand their power and influence by remembering Dominic Cummings, who was chief adviser to Boris Johnson for the first year and a half of his time as Prime Minister. The fact that Cummings was able to call his own press conference in the No. 10 rose garden on a summer afternoon and keep the press waiting until he turned up to explain his trip to Barnard Castle during lockdown, and his total domination of the front pages the next morning and for quite a long time after, demonstrated how the power of the political adviser had grown since Marcia's arrival in No. 10. What she had struggled to do alone had become the job of a large team.

The political papers of Harold Wilson, which now form part of the Bodleian Library's special collection, highlight the work Marcia did as a devoted and very hard-working controller of affairs in the constituency, the House of Commons and the Labour Party. In the early years in government, Marcia wrote letter after letter to Harold's constituents, often with two or three follow-ups if the problem was a tough one. They are all there, the typewritten carbon copies from the personal and political secretary to the Prime Minister, often with questions and notes to the Prime Minister in Marcia's hand.

Letters from the people of Ormskirk and later Huyton often began 'Dear Harold' and mention that the writer had met the Prime Minister or at least caught a glimpse of him at some local function.

Dear Mr Wilson,

I am writing this letter to ask your advice. My wife and I and all our family were banned for life from the Kirby Library and also brought to court for damage to library books. We did no damage to the books. The court found us not guilty and dismissed the case. I am an ex-regular soldier and would like to know why myself and my family were banned from the library before our case came to court. I was led to understand that a person in this country was innocent until proved guilty. We were found not guilty yet we were banned for life before the court hearing. Also as a man with an unblemished character, my name was published in the paper before the case came up.

Sincerely,

(Sgt) J. Platt

Over fifty years ago, Marcia did all the research and was able to write back and assure Sergeant Platt that a terrible mistake had been made and the Prime Minister had been able to clear the family's name with the local authorities and a letter of apology from them was on the way.

As the wife of a backbench MP in the 1970s, I can recognise the key role Marcia was playing in Downing Street. Dozens of letters came in every week, each one requiring research and a reply, and Marcia did it all meticulously and often with humour or sympathy, whichever was required, building solidly over the years Harold Wilson's reputation as a reliable and trustworthy constituency MP and a Prime Minister who was personally helping all his own constituents to resolve their problems.

In 1964, as a woman, and a Labour woman, there was no precedent

Marcia could use to argue her case and make people respect the importance of her role. She saw herself as chief adviser to Harold, but she was going to have to fight for it.

I asked Professor Jon Davis, head of the Strand Group at King's College and an expert in central government, how tough it would have been for Marcia trying to establish herself as the first female political secretary and special adviser in Downing Street:

I think it was George Brown who first described special advisers as irregulars. There were none after the Second World War, however there were one or two characters like John Wyndham under Harold Macmillan who were advisers in Downing Street.

They weren't civil servants, they weren't politicians, and they paid for themselves.

Many Westminster watchers and insiders believe Britain is a conservative country that occasionally votes Labour. There can be long gaps, thirteen years in this case between one Labour administration and the next. When Harold Wilson came in, he had nothing to fall back on, and a similar situation arose in 1997.

Professor Davis continues:

Ed Balls told me why he thought special advisers were much more needed under Labour than under the Conservatives, because when Conservatives were truly conservative with a small c, there was a natural affinity with the civil service.

When a radical administration comes in as with Wilson in 1964 you have got to bring in your own people at the top and that is exactly what Harold Wilson did with Balogh, Kaldor and

Neild. But if you are also bringing in a woman in the political
secretary role that is on top of just being a special adviser, the role
that Douglas Hurd had provided for Edward Heath. Now a Prime
Minister can do pretty much whatever they want, but if they want
things to run smoothly and every Prime Minister wants that, to
have an outsider who is also a woman pushed into that role there
was always going to be problems. There was always going to be
friction whoever it was going to be.

Marcia had a very clear idea of how tough it had been when she
talked to Austin Mitchell in 1996:

If you are political and you are going in there, you better be prepared because there will be no help there for you just because you
happen to have a nice face. You have to have influence in the right
areas. That will be difficult. If you want to establish how you are
going to be as a party not just as a government, you are going to
have to make that known from day one.

It is no good expecting it to come to you two or three months
later. From day one, you have to start in there and know what
you are going to do. We knew we had to have a political office.
We knew whatever else happened, the party had to have as much
access to the Prime Minister as the civil servants had. That we
achieved. I don't know whether it could be done now. As they
don't have any access in opposition, I doubt if they will have any
access in government. You don't come risen from the waves like
Venus. You are a party-supported person – you are there by virtue
of being a member of the party, New or Old Labour, and you owe

your allegiance to the other members. You owe them the respect that they deserve, and they get very upset if they don't get that, and they are right. They are right to expect that if they are working themselves to a standstill for you, that when you are a Member of Parliament you won't just disappear into the blue yonder and not even leave a note on a pin cushion for them. That's too much. They will become disaffected. Equally, the Prime Minister mustn't disappear; he must be there so that either he or someone close to him will listen to your grumbles, masses of grumbles from disaffected members of the Parliamentary Labour Party wanting the Vietnam War stopped or saying pensions should have been increased more dramatically or complaining that the party was not behaving properly. It's endless.

Marcia's battle with the civil servants to win acknowledgement of her own role as Harold Wilson's political chief of staff was an issue before she even arrived in the building. Derek Mitchell had replaced Sir Timothy as the man in charge in Downing Street. Ben Pimlott, who interviewed Mitchell for his biography of Wilson, revealed that this most eloquent and formal of civil service bosses, with whom Marcia was soon at war, was in his private and personal life a Labour voter. From the way things developed, it is a safe bet that Marcia never knew that.

On her visit before the election, Marcia had decided that the waiting room next to the Cabinet office where Prime Ministers traditionally worked would be the best place for her to keep her eye on Harold and the men who were so keen to take him over. She instructed him to fix it with Sir Derek.

'When Harold sat down to get on with the work in hand he said, "Let Marcia have the waiting room for her office." So I went there and took possession – and waited,' wrote Marcia.

These days ministers and Prime Ministers are surrounded by spads (special advisers), and it is their job to deal with the political aspects of their bosses' heavy workload. Everything else in government business is the responsibility of the civil servants. There were no special advisers in Downing Street in the 1960s. Douglas Hurd had been the political secretary to Edward Heath, and Marcia would have been happy to do the same job for Harold, but the civil servants disagreed.

After he had talked with the new Prime Minister, Derek Mitchell called Marcia in for a meeting. They tried and failed to come up with a plan for Marcia's role at No. 10. What should her title be? What work would she do? They couldn't agree.

Then there was a discussion with Harold 'as to what my exact title was to be. Private secretary would have been perfectly correct, but this was objected to, though I was qualified academically by private office No. 10 standards,' wrote Marcia huffily, but principal private secretaries, the men who ran the Prime Minister's office, were civil servants, and Marcia was a university graduate with a secretarial qualification, just like many of the Garden Room Girls. The fact that Marcia and Harold had been working so closely together for a decade meant nothing to Derek Mitchell and his colleagues at No. 10.

Marcia recalled:

No one would give us anywhere to work; we had to fight our way into every room. Looking back, I think that after thirteen years of being with the Conservatives, and working so closely with them, the advent of a Labour government was something that was not really palatable or nice. They didn't like the thought of all these socialists coming in and taking over the building and there was an atmosphere. Usually, you are clapped when you win an election. Staff line up and clap you in. When we went in in '64, no one clapped us because no staff lined up. When we went in in '66 with a ninety-six majority, they clapped us wildly.

Civil servants are judging, how stable? How long? Looking at us they might have thought, 'Well, these people might not be here more than a couple of months, so we might have to do it all again, and then our former people might be back and we might have done some awful things and get into trouble,' so they remain neutral. I don't think they were hostile, but they were not going to move, their faces were expressionless, it was an unpleasant atmosphere, no one will convince me other than the way I remember it – it was cold, unfriendly and not very helpful.

By 1964, women in the top rank of the civil service, 'principal private secretary', numbered just two and they were on a different pay scale from their male colleagues. Dame Evelyn Sharp was appointed in 1955, Dame Mary Smieton in 1959. They didn't achieve equal pay with their male colleagues for another twenty years, and until 1946, women who married had to leave the civil service. Female civil servants of executive rank were totally banned from the foreign arm, the diplomatic service.

Lord Butler, then a junior civil servant at No. 10, said that women had fared better in the civil service than in other professions but that this had been helped by the war because so many men were away fighting and so was not necessarily indicative of a permanent change in societal attitudes towards women in work, and particularly women in politics.

There had been eighty-nine female candidates for 650 constituencies in the 1964 election, just eleven won seats for the Conservative Party, and eighteen became Labour MPs. In a house of 650 members of Parliament, there were just thirty-nine women.

It's easy to see that in 1964 the idea of opinionated women in Parliament, in the civil service and, particularly, as the right-hand woman and confidante of the Prime Minister could be a great concern to the 100 per cent male group of top civil servants whose job it was to surround and advise the new Prime Minister.

Of course, there was no mention of the fact that Marcia was a woman – they were far too polite for that – but suspicion and outright hostility to women in Westminster and Whitehall made the situation a lot more difficult than it had been for Edward Heath and Douglas Hurd.

For example, in 1966 Shirley Williams MP was appointed by Harold as a junior minister in the Department of Labour and had her appointment opposed by Sir James Dannett, the permanent secretary in her department. He didn't succeed in getting rid of her, but he refused to communicate with her directly on any matter. Their relationship remained like that until they both moved on to other posts in separate ministries. This was two years after Marcia arrived in Downing Street.

At No. 10, Derek Mitchell proposed that Marcia should be called 'personal and political secretary to the Prime Minister', avoiding the key word 'private', which was strictly reserved for the civil servants.

Marcia wrote:

I eventually left No. 10 at 10 p.m. to return to my home in Golders Green, having been up a very long time and not having had a proper meal in twenty-four hours.

I was too tired that particular day to consider all the implications of what had happened to me. I said to myself: 'I have an office and I have a title. But have I any work to do now?'

Derek Mitchell was a dogged defender of the border between political and official duties. Civil servants were the officials who dealt with the real business of government; people from political parties were another matter. He had refused to allow the presence of Conservative speechwriters in No. 10 to help Douglas-Home. He was to fight similar battles with Marcia over which papers she should see, access to the photocopier and even payment for telephone bills. On one memorable occasion early in their relationship, he told Marcia she could only travel to the USA on the Prime Minister's plane if Mary Wilson was in attendance and Marcia could be justified as Mrs Wilson's maid. As a stickler for the rules, Mitchell made sure that his views on Marcia and her part in the work of Downing Street were kept strictly private, but thirty years later he gave the game away when he was interviewed by Professor Jon Davis, then a PhD student, for his thesis 'Prime Ministers and Civil Service Reform 1960–1974'. Derek Mitchell said of Marcia:

She had the skills of a good constituency secretary ... She could see the politics of any situation and understand it. If a situation required statesmanship instead of simple political nous she was lost. It was beyond her. Not a great brain. Not a [Alastair] Campbell or a [Peter] Mandelson. Nowhere near it, but it was coupled with the deep suspicion she felt more strongly than anyone else who worked with [Harold] that there was this great conspiracy, that all of Whitehall was against him and it was up to the likes of her, all too few of them, to save him somehow and bring him through this. Dreadful situation. A bit weird.

It was a key thought but wrong. If a man and a woman in politics were working together as closely and effectively as Harold and Marcia, it should have been obvious that both were contributors to one cause. Proud and supportive mothers like Harold Wilson's had given up their own advancement for their sons in the early twentieth century, because no one could yet visualise smart women in leading roles. But in the late 1950s, Marcia's husband Ed believed Marcia saw her job with Harold as a stepping stone to a parliamentary seat. He had written to his in-laws in the early days of their marriage: 'I think she is bound to end up in the House of Commons sooner or later and as far as having a family is concerned, I think the sooner the better.'

It was not to be. What Ed was suggesting was the route followed by Margaret Thatcher, a politician of the next generation whose twins were six when she arrived in the Commons.

But just like Harold's mother had done before her, Marcia provided Harold with all the flair, support, good ideas and connections with the real world that he could never have managed on his own. Harold Wilson had become the Prime Minister in equal part because of his brilliance and ideas and the enormous contribution of Marcia, a woman who instinctively understood politics and quickly became an expert adviser to the man at her side. She didn't defer to him because he was the boss because she didn't see him that way. As far as she was concerned, they were political partners, two halves of one operation, and she had a clear contribution to make which would underpin his and ensure the progress of this new Labour government.

But until the day Harold resigned, most of the men and many of the women who surrounded Marcia and Harold couldn't understand this. The universal question they all asked was why did she boss him around and bully him? She was only his secretary; why couldn't she behave like one? Many men – including Joe Haines, who came in to run the press office just before Labour lost the 1970 election, and Dr Joe Stone, Harold's medical adviser – believed Marcia was a block on the road to progress. If Harold could only get rid of Marcia, they believed, he would become and be seen as a truly great Prime Minister. But they were wrong. From the beginning, and particularly in the first fourteen years she worked with Harold, Marcia was an equal partner.

She believed she was, and Harold encouraged her. From the moment his mother died of cancer in 1957 and missed seeing her son become Prime Minister, until the day he died three decades later, Marcia was Harold Wilson's political mainstay and chief supporter.

George Wigg, the MP who had run Harold's successful campaign to become leader the Labour Party and was made Paymaster General in the new government, adopted the same patronising tone that Derek Mitchell had when he first met Marcia in Downing Street.

In his autobiography, published in 1972, George Wigg described Marcia was 'a competent shorthand typist with a degree' and that was the beginning but not quite the end of it.

Like every energetic secretary she became increasingly accustomed to taking day-to-day decisions on behalf of her employer. Now ensconced in No. 10 it seemed to me she failed to realise that action on behalf of the Prime Minister was very different from the business of working for the Leader of the Opposition. She now gradually came to take on responsibilities which I thought extended beyond those appropriate to a personal secretary and to behave towards myself, among others, as if she were a political force in her own right and a power to be reckoned with.

Wigg managed to sum up in one pompous and misogynist paragraph just how tough it was for women to establish themselves back in the 1960s. And lest you think he was yet another old-school Colonel Blimp, just a couple of pages later he reinforced his fears for the future of the government:

> The influence exerted by Mrs Williams inside No. 10 was great and pervasive, for there was no doubt the Prime Minister rated her opinions as important and on many issues her reaction markedly influenced his thinking. Although I kept as far away from Mrs Williams as possible, clashes were inevitable. I remember an encounter between Mrs Williams, Harold Wilson and myself. I wished to raise a matter of a confidential nature. I told Wilson I would not talk about it in front of Mrs Williams. Wilson courteously asked her if she would mind leaving. She flounced out, obviously in a very bad temper.

Wigg decided that the civil servants and ministerial colleagues had a formidable competitor for the Prime Minister's ear. 'Her growing influence was not always exercised with wisdom and discretion.

It often disturbed the very competent private office in No. 10 and spread unease among men and women of great ability and complete loyalty.'

Harold and Marcia saw eye to eye over Wigg: he had quickly become a menace. He had started out as a member of the Kitchen Cabinet, and Harold enjoyed and found useful the gossip and stories that Wigg came up with, but he was better tolerated at a distance and was moved to an office at 70 Whitehall.

Marcia's problems with the civil servants who formed the private office and worked with the Prime Minister had to be taken more seriously. By the time Harold and Marcia arrived in Downing Street, every civil servant who worked there had told someone the joke that the previous Prime Minister Harold Macmillan, having lunch at the Beefsteak Club, had remarked, 'Funny fellow, Harold Wilson. I hear he keeps his mistress in Downing Street. I always kept mine in St John's Wood.'

But to Harold and Marcia, arriving in No. 10 must have felt like the new beginning of everything they had worked for together.

What the civil servants failed to see was that Marcia was absolutely essential to Harold. A non-negotiable part of his premiership. She had an acute political brain capable of testing and managing his and a powerful ability to cut her way through the vagueness and waffle of political argument to get to the heart of an issue.

Sexual intercourse had ended long before 1963 and the Beatles' first LP. Harold and Marcia had worked together closely for years to achieve this moment. The first Labour government for thirteen years. There had been no criticisms, no hissy fits, no inability to cope from either of them. They believed that they had planned a new future for Britain together.

Of course, there had been plenty of gossip at Labour Party HQ and in Parliament. What observer, seeing the couple chatting closely together, night after night always at a table for two in the Commons cafeteria, when ordinary workers were back home with their families, didn't speculate as to how close that relationship really was?

When they first arrived at No. 10, Marcia and Harold were untroubled by outsiders about personal relationships. What happened in Downing Street stayed in Downing Street. The press, radio and now television conscientiously ignored or covered up the day-to-day lives of those in the public eye. They'd been doing it that way for ever.

But inside No. 10, the relationship with Derek Mitchell, the chief personal private secretary to the Prime Minister, which had smouldered through the planning stages as he and Marcia discussed offices she might use, the job title she might have and the work she was going to do, burst into flames. Marcia was as nervous about the civil servants as they were about her:

> I had no guidance. When it was government policy, it had nothing to do with me. I had no connection whatever except that I was working in the building and knew what was happening and had to be told for the purposes of political liaison. I didn't have any role in the private office in that sense. My work was to make sure that the link with the Labour Party was preserved, that MPs, when they wanted, could have access to the Prime Minister and they could come and complain as they had in his eighteen months as Leader of the Opposition. This was something Gaitskell had never done. Gaitskell did not have an open-door policy for MPs. Harold had a totally open-door policy. They could wander in

and if he was not free they were given a time to come back and see him. They were never refused. We wanted to keep that going afterwards, so that they had the same feeling of being able to approach him, and we wanted to make sure that the party could too. So I organised all of that. I actually got a new room fitted out and equipped in the House of Commons so that it could be done in the Palace of Westminster as well without having the civil service take over and, not knowing people, keep them out.

One of the problems for the civil service in a takeover is that they are very familiar with the party in government but they are not at all familiar with the people in opposition, so when a whole lot of new faces start turning up, they turn them away. They say things like, 'This funny man came in today...' and you discover that this was the chairman of the Parliamentary Labour Party who's just been sent packing.

Marcia was determined that civil servants were not going to come between her and Harold, so she was brave and forthright and, it seems, 'shouty' in setting out her grounds.

We'd be right to blame her if she tried that approach now. Women have learned a great deal about how to behave in the office in the past fifty years. Back then when even the most sympathetic of men interrupted you, pinched your ideas if not your bum and loudly talked over you to explain the point you were making, brave women stiff with fear and nervous of losing control shouted down their male opponents to make their points, and Marcia certainly acted forcefully with Derek Mitchell and the civil servants in No. 10.

It's taken both men and women a long time to learn. In 1997, with all the excitement of Blair's Babes arriving in Westminster, Tony

Blair was fine dealing with the middle-class women who joined his government and worked in his office, but he was nervous and puzzled with the women like Marcia who took a more aggressive stance. Mo Mowlam and Clare Short stood up to Blair and he reacted badly to their forceful approaches. There were times when Mowlam was left out of the negotiations in Northern Ireland, and Short sometimes argued her point too loudly and forcefully for Blair to be convinced she was the right minister for the job.

Ben Pimlott says Marcia saw herself as the new Prime Minister's political arm. The civil servants wanted Harold to get on with running the country or at least to agree to them doing it in his name, but Marcia wanted him to remember who'd put him in No. 10 and who he was working for.

Marcia was also worried about how she was perceived in No. 10. She knew the Garden Room Girls didn't like her, and she made it clear that she didn't approve of them. They'd all been privately educated (just like her) and were graduates of the poshest secretarial college, St Godric's in Hampstead (just like her).

Margarete, Tony Field's widow, told me that Tony had paid for Marcia to go to St Godric's. He was always generous to his unmarried sisters, she said, helping them to get on.

Margarete also told me, and it seems appropriate to mention it here, that the Field family had a pet name for Marcia when she was a little girl: Napoleon. Her father had always believed she was a great strategist who would stop at nothing to get her way.

The civil servants began to realise that Harold Wilson depended on Marcia, practically, psychologically and intellectually.

After a year in No. 10, Richard Crossman noted: 'She still is the most influential figure in Harold's life.'

Wilson himself said, 'She has stuck by me through thick and thin. If I get thrown out of here, she will still be my supporter.'

The threatened rail strike of February 1965 cheered up the political office. Suddenly, they were involved in something which was happening downstairs. The railwaymen came to No. 10 for discussions and stayed late into the night. Sandwiches were provided by the private office. They had been ordered from government hospitality and were very small and dainty. Marcia and her staff went shopping and fed the railwaymen plenty of beer and solid food. They also took over the job of delivering it to the Cabinet Room because Marcia had noticed that every time the civil servants went into the room, the talking dried up. 'The end result was a successful one and we were euphoric when we saw them on their way in the early hours of the morning,' wrote Marcia.

Immediately after Christmas, Harold Wilson decided he wanted to have a general election in March, but before that he, Marcia and Mary along with Alun Chalfont (a Foreign Office minister) and Frank Cousins (boss of the Transport and General Workers' Union, Britain's most powerful trade union) went to Moscow.

In her book *Inside Number 10*, Marcia reports that she and Mary were amazed at a conversation they had had in Russia with Frank Cousins about equal pay. Marcia and Mary were of course both in favour, but 'Frank denounced our views as quite unacceptable, and said he totally disagreed with the whole principle'. He was forced to change his views when 200 female workers at the Ford plant in Dagenham came out on strike just a couple of years later and equal pay became law in 1970.

On 28 February 1966, Harold Wilson announced a general election in four weeks' time.

'My first instruction to everyone was to pack everything ready to move at a moment's notice. All our box files were tied together, our desks were emptied and our books made ready to move,' Marcia recalled.

But it soon became obvious as the Labour caravan trailed all over the country, most often by sleeper, that Britain was changing and there was goodwill for Harold and his team. Harold's best friends including Joseph Kagan all turned up in Harold's suite at the Adelphi in Liverpool to share in the celebrations.

Marcia reminisced:

Our arrival at No. 10 was extraordinary. Extraordinary because it was so totally different from 1964. There was Michael Halls, with his bright smiling face, beaming his congratulations and the rest of the staff all lined up and clapping.

We didn't feel the world was our oyster because we knew with an inward groan that we were going back into politics. Remember this is still the time of Vietnam, still the time of Rhodesia – two world events that were hanging there like black clouds. And the economy. We knew we'd actually been able to make it look good and be very convincing in the election campaign, but there were problems up ahead, particularly with the trade union movement over wages and prices problem. There were difficulties. We knew that they were there. We could feel them. Harold came back into No. 10 and we all went up in the lift together to the flat. He said, 'I think we will just mark time for a little while to recover our strength,' meaning just let it tick over until we can regroup and work out what we want and where we are going. But by the time he sat down to work that out, God knows what happened and all hell broke loose.

9

The Move

BBC Radio 1 began broadcasting at 7 a.m. on 30 September 1967. DJ Tony Blackburn introduced the first disc, 'Flowers in the Rain' by the Move – a song that would come to be central to a public scandal concerning Harold and Marcia's relationship.

The Move were a collection of talented Birmingham lads – Roy Wood, Trevor Burton, Chris 'Ace' Kefford, Carl Wayne and Bev Bevan, brought together from other pop groups: Nightriders, the Mayfair Set, Idle Race and Carl Wayne & the Vikings. Hence, the Move.

'Flowers in the Rain' was number two in the pop charts when it made history as the first track ever played on the brand-new Radio 1. The Move were to have nine top-twenty UK singles in five years. The group was headed for stardom and styled themselves as the Midlands' answer to the Who.

Roy Wood was the lead singer and composer of 'Flowers in the Rain' and many of their other hits. Moody Blues manager Tony Secunda took them on and got them a weekly booking at famous venue, the Marquee Club, in 1966.

Secunda had a reputation for being wild. He was reckless and daring and dreamed up mad stunts. When the Roundhouse opened to bands, the Move took part in a 'Giant Freak-Out All Night Rave' called Psychedelicamania to celebrate New Year's Eve in 1966.

With Roy Wood's prolific talent for song writing, news of the exciting new band spread quickly. It wasn't long before they were offered a recording contract by producer Denny Cordell. The offer was accepted, and Secunda had the contract drawn up on the bare back of topless model Liz Wilson. Appropriate photographs with the lads of the Move, all eyes to the front, featured Miss Wilson's shapely back and the lovingly handwritten contract details.

Then, with Secunda hell-bent on publicity, any publicity, the group began to include violent onstage acts to their musical performances. Carl Wayne regularly took an axe to television sets on stage. Sometimes the group chopped holes in the floor beneath them. All this climaxed the night Carl Wayne destroyed a working Cadillac on stage with an axe and a chainsaw. Alarm bells were rung and Soho became jammed with fire engines for hours. Some young women found the event so stressful that they tore off their tops and enjoyed the rest of the event naked to the waist. For a few weeks at least the Move were banned from every top music venue in London.

Meanwhile, Tony Secunda, without bothering to consult any of his band members who were on tour at the time, decided to promote 'Flowers in the Rain' with a postcard. Cartoonist Neil Smith produced a black and white drawing of Harold Wilson and Marcia Williams in bed together. Five hundred copies, which included in the artwork the words 'disgusting, depraved, despicable' in fat curly letters, were posted out.

Looking at it over fifty-five years later, it's hard to see any connection at all between the postcard of Harold and Marcia and 'Flowers in the Rain', but Secunda seemed to believe outrage was the key to good publicity, and outrageous it certainly was.

So, the Prime Minister of the United Kingdom Harold Wilson sued Essex boy Anthony Secunda, all the members of the Move, the cartoonist Neil Smith and the printers in the High Court.

Strictly non-politically, the Prime Minister was represented by the shadow Home Secretary Quintin Hogg QC, who had himself made veiled references to an affair between Harold and Marcia years earlier during a general election campaign.

In court, Quintin Hogg said that the Prime Minister's reputation had been damaged by the malicious rumours which had been circulated about his private life and integrity. The postcard which had been posted openly, not even in an envelope, to disc jockeys, journalists and television producers had made use of the rumours about him which Wilson had always considered it right to treat with the contempt they deserved.

'But in the present instance the scurrility of the card coupled with the extent of the circulation and threatened circulation left him with no alternative but to assert his legal rights and thereby to make plain his determination to establish the complete falsity of these rumours,' Hogg said.

Harold Wilson won the court case. All his costs were to be paid.

In addition to the agreed payments, the defendants were required to submit to an injunction for life. The court decreed that the royalties on the record and sheet music of 'Flowers in the Rain', and the B-side 'Lemon Tree', were to go into a trust and the money was to be shared equally between two charities chosen by Wilson: the Spastics Society (which years later became Scope) and the amenity funds of Stoke Mandeville Hospital, to aid paraplegic patients.

At the time, James Loring, director of the Spastics Society, said: 'We are tremendously grateful for the Prime Minister's generous and thoughtful gesture. The society is at present facing a grave financial crisis.' Apparently, the society stood to lose up to a quarter of a million pounds annually as a result of a court decision on the tax liability of its football pool, a major source of the charity's income.

When Harold Wilson died in 1995, members of the Move applied to the courts for the injunction to end, but this was refused. The only change was that Marcia, now Baroness Falkender, would choose the charities which would benefit from the royalties.

When Baroness Falkender died in 2019, the story of Harold, Marcia and the Move was revisited by Craig Brown in the *Daily Mail*. Brown estimated that Roy Wood and his fellow band members had lost a quarter of a million pounds in royalties to Harold Wilson's charities in the fifty-two years since the court case.

Craig Brown used the opportunity to run through all the early accusations against Marcia.

'Might it have been Marcia who put Harold up to suing the Move, even though they both knew the cartoon to be true?'

Could the Prime Minister have perjured himself in court to put paid to the rumours?

Quintin Hogg had said in court that Wilson had agreed to the terms of settlement which might be thought extremely generous.

In view, however, of the wide dissemination of the postcard, he wishes me to make it quite clear that he would not necessarily take the same lenient view of any subsequent occasion. Indeed, in the opinion of his advisers, the character of the libel was such as to warrant criminal proceedings.

These days suing people for reputational damage has lost the power it had in the 1960s. The iron grip of proprietors on newspapers before social media began meant that people with influence could protect their secrets from public attention unless they appeared in the pages of the new and increasingly powerful *Private Eye*. The Move postcard went to only a maximum of 500 addressees, and over the years it has certainly lost its power to shock. In 2023, Pauline Evans, who had run the Move's fan club and been for a while the girlfriend of Carl Wayne, found her own copy of the postcard in a chest of drawers at home. She took it to Fieldings Auctioneers in Stourbridge. They gave it a lot of publicity and the *Daily Mail* retold the story, but the postcard didn't meet its reserve of £1,000 and went home again to Pauline Evans's bottom drawer.

Throughout Marcia's lifetime, suing people was to become an important feature of her public persona. Joe Haines was often to report that after an angry tirade about her latest enemy, she would tap her handbag as if it held precious evidence, and announce that she would sue.

Dr Joe Stone lived in fear that Marcia would insist on taking someone to court. He believed her temperament was so mercurial that without considerable medical help (i.e. tranquillisers), she would be out of control and wreck the Prime Minister's reputation. After the Move court case, people at Westminster wondered if Marcia had persuaded Harold to sue the Move. It was just another version of the old story that she had some powerful hold over him and wasn't about to let go.

10

Constructing a Reputation

Today, Marcia Williams is remembered by many as the woman who screamed and shouted at Prime Minister Harold Wilson. But how did this reputation develop?

At seventeen, Marcia's school friend Ann Cauldwell described her as clever, friendly and hard-working with a passion for show-business. And once Marcia started working at Westminster and with the Labour Party, colleagues thought she was super-smart and efficient.

Marcia only began to face difficulties and develop a reputation for eccentric behaviour when she and Harold arrived in No. 10 after Labour won the 1964 election with a majority of just four. Marcia's first serious problem came from the civil servants who believed, as they always had, that it was their job to take any new Prime Minister firmly in hand and bend him to their will.

The relationships between ministers and civil servants were clear and undisputed in the 1960s. Civil servants in Downing Street were there to advise the Prime Minister, help him choose the best path for the government to pursue and implement it on his behalf.

Marcia believed the civil servants wanted to capture the Prime Minister for themselves and get back to running the country. She wanted them to acknowledge that theirs was only half the job, and that she and Harold had another role: running the Labour Party, managing Labour MPs and dealing with the voters who made direct contact with their elected representatives personally. In those days that would have meant letters to the MPs and to the Prime Minister himself, or attendance at MPs' 'surgeries' in constituencies across Britain. Marcia wanted Harold to acknowledge who it was who had made him leader of the Labour Party, won the election and put him in 10 Downing Street, and even in those early days she wanted him to stand up to the civil servants on her behalf.

The much-loved television series *Yes Minister*, which began in 1980 just four years after Harold Wilson resigned as Prime Minister, centred on the relationships between civil servants and ministers. Week after week, viewers enjoyed the smooth-talking Sir Humphrey's skills in hoodwinking minister and then Prime Minister Jim Hacker MP. The civil servants led Hacker to believe he was in charge and running his department when the truth was always the opposite. In the show, civil servants ruled the roost as they always had, and they always won in the end.

In real life, Derek Mitchell tried Sir Humphrey's technique on Marcia after the 1964 election victory. She refused to be cowed. Mitchell and his staff were misogynistic, patronising her, but she fought back. They attempted to get rid of her and failed. Mitchell tried to dismiss her as a constituency secretary type with not much more to offer. But Harold Wilson began as he meant to go on and supported Marcia's demands for a place for politics and a proper political office inside No. 10.

The civil servants were forced to tolerate Marcia's presence from the moment Labour arrived.

She was a major irritant, always by Harold's side listening, cautioning and advising him, but no one called her unstable, controlling, hysterical or unhinged. All that had to wait for the arrival of Joe Haines as Wilson's press secretary at the end of the 1960s.

The son of a hospital cleaner and a Rotherhithe dockworker, Joseph Haines was fourteen when he began his newspaper career on the Glasgow *Bulletin* and was in his forties when he arrived at No. 10, after climbing the ladder as a political journalist in Fleet Street. Joe then spent the prime of his life working with Marcia and Harold, and after Harold Wilson's retirement, Joe joined another legend, Robert Maxwell, at Mirror Group Newspapers. Joe was, and still is today at ninety-five, tough, opinionated, rigidly truthful and judgemental. He observed closely the complex relationship that had built up between Harold and Marcia, dominating their lives in public and in private, and he thought deeply about it, wrote about it and, it's fair to say, became obsessed with it. His first book, *The Politics of Power*, was published in 1977 when James Callaghan was Prime Minister. It is an informative and very readable account of how Downing Street worked in the 1960s and '70s. Marcia rated a chapter in this first book and Joe rated Marcia. He acknowledged how clever and politically astute she was and the key role she played in getting Harold elected as leader of the Labour Party and winning two general elections. Joe noted how close the pair were and might well have dubbed them 'better together'.

'It is impossible to judge Wilson's record and reputation without encompassing Marcia's role,' he says. 'The youthful Marcia focused Wilson on the ultimate objective. Gave him direction, made him shed his grey image and sharpened his speeches. She can claim to have moulded the man he had become.'

Joe continued: 'Wilson depended on her practically, psychologically and intellectually.'

Joe also wrote approvingly of Marcia's early wrangles with the civil servants who ran Downing Street, noting her clear thinking. He acknowledged that she'd had an impossible relationship with Derek Mitchell and that within a few weeks of her arrival there had been open warfare between them. Joe the fighter admired Marcia the fighter who saw herself as the leader of the new Prime Minister's political wing.

Nearly thirty years later, however, Joe wrote *Glimmers of Twilight: Harold Wilson in Decline*. The book's title comes from a line in Robert Browning's poem 'The Lost Leader'. Browning was writing about William Wordsworth, who he believed had deserted the liberal cause. In the book, Joe sets out to blame what he saw as Wilson's decline on 'the tantrums, tirades and tyranny of Marcia Williams'. He was positively vitriolic about her personality and the way he felt she dominated Harold. He has a passionately held belief that she is the keeper of a terrible secret which caused her many times in the Downing Street days to tap loudly on her handbag as if the truth was hidden in the lining to be revealed by her when the moment was right. Joe points out that he was not jealous of Marcia or her closeness to Harold, and he puts himself forward as the best judge of what happened to Wilson and the Labour Party in the 1970s, because he was there at the Prime Minister's side, with a front-row seat as history was being made.

Joe explains that he waited until Wilson and his close friend and personal doctor Lord Joseph Stone were dead before he told his story fully. He said that in his previous book, published just after Wilson's retirement, he had put a gloss on the truth. He said it hadn't seemed right to focus on the private relationship between the main characters. I suspect it's more likely that no one would have published it. In the 1970s, journalists were still expected to put a gloss on certain grades of truth. The private lives of living politicians and millionaires largely stayed private. Powerful proprietors demanded it. Only *Private Eye* did things differently.

Private Eye began in 1961 and grew to great strength and began to reach a much wider audience during Harold Wilson's time as Prime Minister. Marcia loathed and feared the magazine, the first to reveal details of her sexual relationship with the political editor of a popular newspaper and her resulting pregnancies. She believed from the beginning of her time in Downing Street that the truth about her unusual private life must be hidden at all costs. It was only after she became Baroness Falkender that *The Times* published a detailed and critical biography of her, and the *Sunday Telegraph*, in a cover story, portrayed her as a glamorous but penurious society figure who did the school run during the week, before going on to do a day's work at Westminster. At the weekends, she went to her country house in the home counties not far from the Prime Minister's.

Then a valuable new source of information about Marcia and her private life at Westminster appeared with the arrival of Bernard Donoughue, who was appointed head of Harold Wilson's newly formed policy research unit. He was in place for the 1974 election campaign. Bernard decided that he would keep a diary of his time in No. 10. He wasn't quite sure what he would do with it, but from the moment he arrived, he sat down at the end of every day and recorded what had been happening.

Like many others who made it in politics and the civil service in the 1970s, Bernard was a clever grammar school lad who had been to Oxford, emerged with first-class honours and was teaching at the London School of Economics when he was recommended to the Prime Minister. His contribution to the story of Marcia, *Downing Street Diary: With Harold Wilson in No. 10*, was not published until 2005. He explains in the preface: he told no one he was keeping a diary, but he decided after finishing it in 1979 that he would wait at least fifteen years before publishing it, as recommended by the Radcliffe Report on ministerial and official memoirs. 'As the years passed, there always seemed to be reason for a further delay. Throughout the 1990s, I was either a minister or a frontbench spokesman and to me that ruled out publication.' So it was two years after the publication of Joe Haines's explosive book about Marcia's behaviour that Bernard Donoughue's detailed reportage about life in Downing Street in the Wilson years appeared. It is comprised of notebooks hurriedly handwritten by Bernard last thing at night, and every night. He provides excellent raw material on the daily lives of Harold and Marcia and their interactions. His diaries may produce gasps of shock from young women now who find it hard to believe that their mothers and grandmothers, many still with us, were so misunderstood and undervalued by the men in their lives. They are a handy reminder for those of us who lived through those years of how much life has changed since the 1970s.

Bernard Donoughue, like Marcia Williams, was born in Northamptonshire. When he was in the sixth form, his girlfriend Jill Booty was a school mate of Marcia's at Northampton High School.

Bernard said he used to watch Marcia striding through the bus station on her way home after school. Maybe Jill pointed her out. Bernard thought Marcia looked 'posh'. Jill said she was 'remote'. Bernard's diaries reveal him as a much gentler, more sympathetic and less worldly-wise character than Joe Haines.

Bernard described Marcia in his first week working in No. 10:

She is constantly lively and bright and cynically realistic about H. W., knowing all his faults, but seems always loyal and affectionate. Not at all what I expected, apparently a devoted supporter of Roy Jenkins and constantly working to get him and others like Callaghan and Shirley Williams to appear at press conferences. She gets on well with Jenkins's assistant John Harris. Clearly no respecter of the left. Always constructive, looking for decisions, handling people with rather brutal honesty but always gets a solution. A much better politician than H. W. or most other MPs, but sometimes very heavy on fools. Totally lacking in deference towards H. W. Simply tells him the brutal truth as she sees it. E.g. today she told him he must use the shadow Cabinet team and push his colleagues forward. He agreed.

Bernard was always ready to follow to the letter instructions from Harold to lend a hand and help save Marcia from her latest drama. But his diaries record endless arguments between Marcia and Harold, with Bernard spending an incredible number of evenings rushing to her home to intervene in the latest confrontation with the press or hysterical screaming match with the Prime Minister.

On 24 February 1974, Bernard wrote: 'Marcia is really depressed … She took a purple heart earlier to keep awake, as she frequently does, and now has a headache. But her intelligence is undiminished. I can see why H. W. is fascinated by her.'

But it wasn't just young Bernard, fresh from the academic life, who found Marcia so fascinating. Everyone in Downing Street was fascinated by Marcia. As Joe Haines says, 'She never displayed her influence publicly but flaunted it in private. She was known about but hardly known, talked about but seldom talking. Perhaps she saw in Harold a greater opportunity than he did himself. She became more than his secretary. She was his manager and his political wife.'

Joe Haines was right. Marcia and Harold had achieved the prime ministership together. She was an equal partner in all but name at a time when there was no history of, or place for, such an arrangement.

Joe says that until Labour lost the 1970 election, he and Marcia never had a cross word. He confesses that he was totally unaware, along with everyone else in No. 10, that Marcia's life had begun to change dramatically during the 1960s in ways that would affect them all for many years to come and Marcia for ever.

By the late '60s, after Labour's success in the 1966 election, there had been time for some sort of return to normality, the turning down of the 24-hour full-on politicking that had absorbed Marcia and Harold for so long. Her brief marriage had ended in divorce, and she was childless and thirty-four years old. She and Harold were together, all day every day, and absolutely focused on making Britain a better place to live, but Harold had his wife Mary and their two sons upstairs to go home to, a settled family life of which Marcia was no part. She tried hard enough; she did everything she could to play a part. She held the cheque books, she paid the utility bills for the Wilsons as well as her own. When they needed somewhere to live in a hurry after Labour was defeated in the 1970 election, it was Marcia who found them temporary accommodation in Westminster, followed by a suitable home to rent in Lord North Street. Marcia, perfect office wife that she was, also had to find money to fund the political office.

But Marcia had no one now but Harold. No private life, and a long journey back to the house she was now sharing with her mum

and her sister Peggy. She wrote to her brother Tony Field, a geologist in the Middle East, and begged him to come back to the UK to
run Harold's office at No. 10. She wanted her family close by.

Margarete, Tony's widow, explains that Tony came back because
Marcia was suddenly in so much personal trouble. Margarete always
stresses that Tony believed he had a duty to look after his mum and
his two sisters, a pact he had made with his dad before he died. So
he came home, and he and Harold hit it off immediately. Tony didn't
stay very long as office manager, but he and Harold became close
friends and played golf together for many years.

Marcia also arranged a job for her sister Peg, helping out Mary
Wilson with her letters and engagements. The entire Field family
was now closely involved with 10 Downing Street.

But Marcia was still lonely and in a very unusual situation being
a woman and the close confidant of the Prime Minister – a situation
that was about to be revealed in *Private Eye*. It wasn't until several
years later that newspaper readers were able to read about Marcia's
sex life on the tabloid front pages.

On 19 April 1974, *Private Eye* published issue 322 and, on page
21, there was a full-page item titled 'Mrs Williams' Dowry'. It was
revealed that Marcia

had started an affair with Walter Terry, then political correspondent of the *Daily Mail* (now Political Editor of the *Daily Express*).
As a result of this affair she became pregnant and had a child
which was born in August 1968. She had secretly assumed the
name of Marcia Williams Terry.

11

Sex in No. 10

Early in her time in Downing Street, Marcia began having an affair with a co-worker, John Schofield Allen. Joe Haines describes him as the most unlikely of lovers: 'sweaty, overweight and married'. Wisely, and encouraged by the Prime Minister and funded by Joe Kagan, a wealthy Yorkshire millowner who frequently helped Harold out financially, Schofield Allen went away to Africa for three months and the affair petered out. He came back and married someone else.

Hurt that he had dumped her, Marcia continued to work long hours for Harold and his government. For a decade, she had spent all her working days and the majority of her time off-duty serving the Labour Party and Harold Wilson. In every way she had been stunningly successful. She had moved from Labour Party head office to the House of Commons as secretary to Harold Wilson, and then in rapid succession he had become shadow Chancellor of the Exchequer and she had masterminded a successful campaign to make him boss of the Labour Party and Leader of the Opposition. She had played a vital role in winning two general elections and she had established herself as a key figure in Downing Street, forcing the civil servants to accept her role as, at the very least, the liaison officer between the Prime Minister and his party, his members of Parliament, his constituents and anyone who wrote directly to the top with a plea for help. With a tiny staff and an unpaid Kitchen Cabinet of advisers, she made a unique solo contribution that has never been matched. She saw a gap in the structure at the top and she plugged it and gradually expanded the power of the political office, which employs dozens of people today. And yet, Labour Party workers and executives who owe her so much seem never to have heard of her or understood how much they owe her. Like so many women of her generation, she gave her all in a support role to the man at the top and got nothing in return.

Labour won the 1966 election with a majority of ninety-eight, and Marcia, who was just thirty-four years old, must have allowed herself the luxury of some time to consider her future. We know that once Harold Wilson had been successfully re-elected, she never seriously considered leaving him for anything or anyone else. Many male advisers to politicians went on to become MPs and, in the case of David Cameron, Prime Ministers themselves. There is no suggestion that Marcia ever considered that course, and in the pre-Thatcher years no one in any party dreamed of a female Prime Minister. By this time, Marcia knew Harold so well that she could see and assess her own contribution. Like in the very best of partnerships, she believed that the two of them together made a very powerful whole. But contributions were never balanced. As Mrs Harris explained so powerfully to Christian Dior, men did what they could and women contributed the rest.

But family was also really important to Marcia and biology – something she couldn't have controlled – may have influenced the dramatic change in her behaviour when Labour was re-elected. After several short and failed relationships, she began a close friendship which turned into a passionate love affair with Walter Terry, chief political correspondent of the *Daily Mail*. He was still living with his wife Mavis and their young son and daughter.

Hot gossip began to spread around Westminster when a journalist arrived one evening with an appointment to see the Prime Minister. In those days before iron gates blocked the end of Downing Street, he noticed Walter Terry's car parked in the street outside with someone inside. He went up and knocked on the window and was shocked and horrified when Walter and Marcia unwrapped themselves from a passionate embrace. The journalist sped into No. 10 for his meeting with the Prime Minister and minutes later a cheery Walter appeared in the Prime Minister's study accompanied by Marcia, and offered, as if it was something he did very frequently, to serve drinks all round.

Marcia's love affair with Walter Terry lasted several years and resulted in the birth of her two sons, born during the 1966 Wilson government – Timothy in 1968 and Daniel just ten months later in 1969. The children arrived unannounced and unacknowledged and for their first five years lived in total secrecy with their mother, their widowed grandmother and aunt Peggy in central London, by which time Walter Terry had left them all and returned to his wife.

Marcia gave birth to her first son just before journalist Joe Haines's arrival as deputy to the press officer at No. 10. She had worked steadily throughout her pregnancy in her office right next to the Cabinet Room, dealing with MPs, trade unionists, civil servants and office staff. But everyone who worked there, including Wilson's Kitchen Cabinet and the Garden Room Girls, claimed to be unaware of her pregnancy. With amazing loyalty to Harold Wilson and the Labour Party, those few who are left now, mostly women who worked closely with Marcia and Harold on the political side, still refuse to comment on what happened back in the 1960s.

In his first book about Downing Street, *The Politics of Power*, Joe Haines told the story of his own amazement and shock when the Prime Minister told him about Marcia's children. Journalist Anne Robinson, who was then a columnist in the *Daily Mirror*, asked Joe how on earth Marcia had managed to keep her secret for so many years. Joe said Marca had always turned up early for meetings, so she was always seated when everyone else arrived, and she always kept her coat on!

Anne Robinson observed wryly that men might have fallen for that, but it would take a woman only a few minutes to work out what was going on if someone had behaved so strangely. And that is certainly true. There are still at least two women alive who worked closely with Marcia in No. 10 and neither of them will talk about her at all. Do they still see the birth of her two children as a shame and a scandal over fifty years later?

Today, just over half of all babies born in England and Wales have unmarried parents, completely erasing the stigma of the 1960s, when it was still shocking and unusual for unmarried women to give birth, keep their babies and bring them up alone. Fewer than 5 per cent of babies were born to unmarried mothers when Marcia gave birth to Timothy in 1968. The 1960s were a time of huge social change in Britain. The pill was made available to married women in 1961 and to all women in 1967, around the same time as abortion was made legal. This was also the beginning of fast-growing demands for equality for women.

But change was hard for older generations and frequently parents disowned their pregnant daughters. Homes for unmarried mothers still flourished across the land. For single women, having babies and keeping them as Marcia Williams decided to do was courageous. But due to societal attitudes, Marcia feared she had to keep her sons secret at all costs. The silence of all concerned at the heart of the British government in the late '6os was by today's standards unbelievable, but the person who paid for it for the rest of their life was Marcia. While many of the wealthy friends she and Harold had made felt sorry for her personally and offered a helping hand, Marcia often felt scared and alone. But she struggled on as a single working mum, always resolutely behind the Prime Minister. He had her total support, and she had his, and that was the part of the story that many men never seemed able to grasp when they began to hate Marcia and try to get rid of her.

The Establishment – the influential and wealthy men who ran Britain – controlled to a very great extent what the rest of the country knew about what was going on at the top. It had taken George Wigg, master of the salacious tale, weeks of careful planning to get the story of War Minister John Profumo's relationship with Christine Keeler discussed in the House of Commons.

Harold Wilson's lawyer Arnold Goodman was in close contact with the proprietors of the Fleet Street newspapers. Those bosses decided what was published and what stayed secret and instructed their editors accordingly. So the story of the birth of Marcia's sons did not see the light of day until *Private Eye* revealed it several years later. The prevention of publication was stressful. Every time a crowd of press people, some of whom worked with Walter Terry and all of whom had heard rumours about Marcia's babies, arrived outside her front door, Marcia became terrified and often hysterical.

On 15 August 1968, Timothy Joseph Henry Williams Terry was born at 46 Sunny Gardens Road, Hendon, in a private hospital specialising in abortions, which had just become legal.

There was a blank space on his birth certificate where it asked for the name of the father. His mother was recorded as Marcia Matilda Williams Terry, a private secretary of 20 Albany Court, Westminster. The informant about the birth was J. Ellis Stone of 615 Finchley Road, who is recorded on the certificate as having been present at the baby's birth.

The informant, who had presumably delivered or supervised the delivery of the baby, was Joseph Stone, the Prime Minister's doctor.

Joseph Ellis Stone (Silverstone) was born in Llanelli in Wales in 1903. He qualified as a doctor at Cardiff University and afterwards at Westminster Hospital Medical School. In those days, Westminster Hospital, on the corner of Horseferry Road and Millbank, was a very short walk from Parliament.

During the Second World War, Joe was a captain in the Royal Army Medical Corps. He was part of the British Army force that liberated Bergen-Belsen concentration camp and was heavily involved as a doctor in rehabilitating the prisoners. He was quite possibly the first British Jewish doctor to enter Belsen.

The journalist Richard Dimbleby was also there and recorded a never forgotten piece for the BBC:

I find it hard to describe adequately the horrible things I have seen and heard but here unadorned are the facts.

There are 40,000 men, women and children in the camp, Germans and half a dozen other nationalities. Thousands are Jews.

Of the total of 40,000, 4,250 are acutely ill or dying of virulent diseases. In the last few months alone, 30,000 prisoners have been killed off or allowed to die. Those are the simple horrible facts of Belsen.

Joseph Stone, a decent warm and compassionate man, must surely have remembered and been affected by those events for ever. His wife Beryl was the sister of Sidney Bernstein who ran Granada Television. Joe's letters to Beryl about what the Royal Army Medical Corps found in Belsen formed part of the research for a Granada Television documentary on concentration camps.

After the war, Joe Stone was a GP in Hendon in north London and he got to know Harold Wilson, when he lived in Hampstead Garden Suburb. They played golf together at the weekends. As soon as Harold became Prime Minister, he appointed his friend Joe as his doctor and medical adviser. They remained strong friends throughout their lives, and during Wilson's time as Prime Minister, Joe travelled the world with him. Joe Stone's loyalty to Prime Minister Harold Wilson was absolute. There is agreement between all those who worked for Harold and Marcia that Dr Stone worshipped Harold. He saw him as a great Prime Minister who was really improving the lives of hard-working families. But it was also acknowledged by the inner circle that Joe Stone loathed Marcia, who he saw as hysterical, according to Joe Haines. Dr Stone believed her closeness to Harold could end only in disaster. But Harold asked Joe Stone to help Marcia, begged him to help sort things out, and Joe knew he had no choice but to agree and to become responsible for her health and welfare. He believed a scandal like Marcia could destroy Harold's premiership.

The arrival of babies, two boys only ten months apart, at the top of the British government, was an unbelievable event for Britain in the 1960s. In those days, the Prime Minister and his wife were a bit like your mum and dad, you knew in your heart that any sex between them had stopped after your arrival. Fecundity at the heart of British government was definitely unheard of even if, or perhaps particularly if, the dad was a *Daily Mail* journalist and the mother the Prime Minister's right-hand woman. If the story of Marcia's babies leaked, said those in the know, who would the world think had fathered them? The obvious, if spurious, choice was Wilson himself, given their close relationship. Such a scandal at the very top of the British government would have rocked the political bedrock.

Around this time, most of the people who surrounded and protected Harold – and were therefore involved in concealing Marcia's pregnancies – were friends he had met away from Westminster, like his golfing buddy and doctor, Joseph Stone. Another close friend and silent witness who turned out to be very important indeed to Marcia was Joseph Kagan, the millowner from Huddersfield, Harold's hometown. Joe Kagan was rich and successful, loyal and sympathetic, and he helped Marcia to buy a flat close to Downing Street in 1967 by providing a deposit and underwriting her mortgage.

In August 1967, the Kagan family were about to go off to Spain on holiday. Just before their departure, Joe called Pauline Windross in to see him privately. Pauline was a local Huddersfield girl and had been nanny to the Kagans' daughter Jenny. She was a capable hard worker and had been promoted. Now she ran a nursery in the Gannex mill for the children of the millworkers. Pauline was loved and trusted by the Kagans, almost a member of the family, and she was due to go with them to Spain on holiday.

Joe, who always had a reputation for kindness and generosity to those who worked for him, told Pauline he needed to ask her a very special favour. If she agreed to his plans, then he was very sorry but she was going to have to miss the family holiday in Spain. Joe explained to Pauline that the Prime Minister, whom Pauline knew because he had visited both the Gannex factory and the Kagans' then home, Delamere in Fixby Road, had someone working very closely with him in 10 Downing Street who required discreet assistance. Marcia Williams was about to have a baby by a newspaper journalist who was married to someone else and the birth had to be kept totally secret because no one knew that she was pregnant and, if the press got whiff of the story, journalists might imply that the baby was the Prime Minister's. Joe highlighted that it definitely was not Harold's baby and that he wanted to protect both Harold and Marcia from the scandal that would ensue if the press discovered Marcia's secret.

Dr Joe Stone had arranged for Marcia to have the baby at an abortion clinic close to his GP practice in Hendon. Back in 1968, mothers stayed in hospital for up to a couple of weeks after the birth of their babies (it was called 'lying in'); they certainly didn't leave for home the next day, or even directly after the baby's birth as Cherie Blair did after the arrival of Leo. There was no way Marcia could stay on in the clinic, so Joe Kagan's plan was for Pauline to go to London and look after Marcia in conditions of great secrecy while the Kagans were in Spain. Margaret Kagan, Joe's wife, owned a flat left to her by her aunt in Marsham Court in Westminster and it had been arranged that Pauline could stay there. Marcia would be in another flat, which Joe had helped her purchase, just above St James's

Park Tube station with her family (mother, father and sister) and the baby. Pauline was to walk to and from Marcia's flat every day and be responsible for the new mother and baby. Marsham Court was just ten minutes' walk away from Marcia's flat, but Pauline would have to travel through the busiest part of Westminster. The streets teemed with politicians, journalists and civil servants. Joe laid out the rules. Pauline was to follow a different route every day to work so that the press didn't follow her. She was to buy the baby's food and other provisions each day in different shops so that no one asked her questions or got to know her and became interested in what she was doing. Pauline, who was excited to be the keeper of such important secrets, agreed to do exactly as she was asked.

When Pauline arrived from King's Cross in a taxi ready to care for Marcia and her baby, Marcia's parents and sister Peggy were already in residence. Pauline thought they were really kind and friendly, and she got on well with them all.

She followed the rules just as Joe had instructed her. One day she would walk along the Embankment, down Victoria Street, stopping at Sainsbury's for her shopping; the next she would make her way to Horseferry Road, picking up her groceries from the Army and Navy Store and crossing into Palace Street to approach St James's Park from a different direction. I asked Pauline if she was ever followed by journalists, and she roared with laughter. 'Of course not!'

And had Dr Stone visited his patient and the new baby? Pauline said that he had. Was he friendly? Well, Pauline didn't really think so. 'Posh, distant,' she concluded. Not the sort to talk to her. Marcia stayed in bed for the two weeks, and Pauline did an excellent job darting between the grocery stores of Westminster and never

Marcia (*background*) and her friend Ann (*right*)
playing croquet on Ann's seventeenth birthday.

When the golden sun is sinking,
    And your mind from care is free.
When of others you are thinking
    Will you sometimes think of me?

Marcia Field
Wednesday
29th March
1944.

Marcia's autograph in Ann's album. They were both passionate movie-goers and wrote
endless letters to their favourite American film stars, hoping to receive autographs.

Prime Minister Harold Wilson and Marcia in Moscow.
© ANL/Shutterstock

A postcard promoting a new single by the Move featured a caricature of Harold and Marcia in bed together. Harold sued for libel and won.
Courtesy of Pauline Pritchard

On the road with the Prime Minister. © PA Images/Alamy Stock Photo

Marcia and Harold working together, preparing notes for the Labour Party conference in 1972.

When Harold made Marcia Baroness Falkender in 1974, *Private Eye* gave her a cover spot and a new title: 'Lady Slagheap', referencing the scandal surrounding her brother's land deals. © *Private Eye*

Listening to the boss at a press conference in Transport House, the Labour Party's head office. © Robert Dear/Associated Press/Alamy Stock Photo

Perfect political partners.
© PA Images/Alamy Stock Photo

Harold with his press secretary Joe Haines (*left*) and head of the policy research unit Bernard Donoughue (*second from right*). © PA Images/Alamy Stock Photo

Marcia with the Who drummer Keith Moon at a charity event. Her passion for show business proved to be everlasting. © Laurence Cotterell/ANL/Shutterstock

Marcia and Harold with Eric Morecambe (*second left*), Marjorie Wilson (*third left*) and David Frost (*second from right*) partying at Downing Street. © Trinity Mirror/Mirrorpix/Alamy Stock Photo

Marcia with Lady Annabel (*second left*), the wife of millionaire London financier Sir James Goldsmith. Goldsmith's appearance on Harold's 1976 resignation honours list fuelled rumours that the so-called 'Lavender List' had been compiled by Marcia rather than by Harold.

© PA Images/Alamy Stock Photo

Marcia and her sons – whose
existence she had tried to keep
secret for many years, fearing
societal backlash because they
were illegitimate – in front of a
framed picture of Harold and
a painting of Westminster.
© Tim Mercer

Marcia visits Harold and
Mary for Sunday lunch
in the country. © Tim Mercer

Lunch in the Lords with Marcia.
© Austin Mitchell

Marcia's last deal: an interview
with the *Mail on Sunday* the
year before she died.
© Craig Hibbert/*Mail on Sunday*

following the same route twice. As good as her word, she travelled back to Elland at the end of the fortnight and returned to her job running the Gannex nursery. Imagine her amazement when just nine months later Joe Kagan asked for another secret meeting.

'It's happened again, I'm afraid,' he said. Just two months after the birth of Timothy, Marcia had gone with Harold to Gibraltar for talks on board the warship HMS *Fearless* about the future of Rhodesia, the southern African country run by Ian Smith's apartheid government. Wilson failed to persuade Smith to end the regime, but both Marcia and Walter Terry had been present (Walter was reporting on the talks for the *Daily Mail*) and Marcia was pregnant again. Could Pauline go back to London and look after the second new baby just like she had the first? Cheerfully, Pauline agreed. This time the conditions were to change. She would go back to the Kagans' flat in Marsham Court and the new baby would stay there with her. Marcia would go back to work.

Daniel Walter Alexander Terry was born on 24 June 1969 at 27 Welbeck Street, these days still a private hospital which seems now to specialise in cosmetic surgery. Both of Daniel's parents signed the birth certificate at Marylebone Registry Office and Daniel was secretly delivered to Pauline at Marsham Court the next day in a cardboard box. Joe Kagan was still very worried about journalists finding out that Marcia had children, so the same rules applied about shopping.

As with the birth of his brother, Daniel had visits from Dr Stone, but it was his father Walter Terry who saw him every day – not his mother. Walter came for an hour and sat with the baby while Pauline did her shopping. Marcia had gone straight back to work.

Today, Pauline and her husband Barry live quietly in a bungalow in Huddersfield. Pauline is still very close to Jenny Kagan and remembers the whole Kagan family as loving and generous. Life was happy and exciting when the Gannex mill was at the heart of her community.

12

The Case of Michael Halls

Michael Halls replaced Derek Mitchell as principal private secretary to the Prime Minister in 1966. Mitchell was the man who had rated Marcia's political skills on a level with a parliamentary secretary of the typing and shorthand kind based in a far-flung constituency. She must have hoped for much better from Michael Halls. Halls had worked with the young Harold Wilson at the Board of Trade. Harold liked him and so did Marcia. Both Harold and Marcia saw Michael as a different kind of civil servant. He wasn't 'posh' like those they already knew and the pair felt he had a lot in common with them, their sense of informality and their working-class values. The new Prime Minister requested that Halls be transferred to Downing Street and so he was, but some of the old civil service hands had grave doubts, thinking Halls was not tough or experienced enough to do the job. Sadly, they turned out to be right, and the incident shone a negative spotlight on Marcia and Harold's relationship.

Halls was the son of an Islington milkman who had begun his civil service career in Customs and Excise while he studied for a law degree at King's College London in the evening. Just before the war, he moved to the Inland Revenue as an assistant tax inspector.

He was already an officer in the territorial army, and during the war he rose to be a lieutenant colonel, having been at Dunkirk and Normandy. He was awarded a military MBE in 1945. After the war, he joined the Board of Trade and met up with the young Harold Wilson, who was president of the board. Halls wasn't popular with his colleagues, who saw him as an over-promoted sycophant. But Wilson liked him from the beginning. Just as he saw himself as different from his Labour frontbench colleagues, he saw Halls as a good straightforward man without the social class and conservative concerns of most of the civil servants around him. Senior officials in Whitehall thought Halls wasn't 'big' enough for the job at Downing Street, but Wilson explained to Sir Laurence Helsby, head of the civil service, that the appointment was not based on Michael Halls's intellectual achievements but the need to ensure that Wilson's office worked efficiently.

Michael Halls immediately demonstrated his commitment to his boss when Marcia complained to him that the Garden Room Girls were far too conservative in their attitudes. She meant conservative with a capital 'C'. She felt they showed what she saw as all the prejudices of educated girls from Establishment families, and when they were 'on the road', they often looked better dressed and more elegant than the members of the public they were supposed to communicate with. Joe Haines reported that Michael Halls under instructions from Marcia made the lives of several of the women a misery by trying to explain all this, until they asked to be moved to other departments. Michael Halls and Marcia appeared to get on well and work smoothly together. Halls told friends how much he enjoyed working for Wilson.

Richard Crossman in his *Diaries* explained: 'He was also naturally attuned with Harold, with the same inhibitions, the same limitations of taste. Harold doesn't really like literature or art, the theatre or the opera. He prefers golf and the telly and the cup final.'

He concluded with a flourish: 'They are both of the petty bourgeoisie.'

During his time at No. 10, Halls joined with the Prime Minister in his attempts to modernise the civil service. He was working on proposals with Lord Armstrong and Lord Crowther Hunt, but in the end he criticised submissions from the civil service department as insufficiently radical.

There is no doubt that Halls was a loyal civil servant devoted to Wilson's government. Harold saw him as a true friend as well as a co-worker. After the birth of Marcia's second son, Harold felt so close to Michael Halls that he confessed the whole story of the affair between Marcia and Walter Terry and swore him to secrecy. Halls was amazed and very shocked. He couldn't quite believe that a sexual relationship, a love affair, between the Labour Prime Minister's political secretary and a senior journalist for a popular right-wing newspaper was possible, or how it could stay a secret. Very worried by Wilson's revelations, he passed on this piece of juicy gossip to his wife. Both, in their different ways, continued to worry about it.

There is solid agreement all round that Halls worked incredibly hard, took his work very seriously and wanted to have a firm grasp on every part of Downing Street's output.

Joe Haines writes that he was amazed to discover that Halls had ordered the Downing Street switchboard to allow him to be patched through so he could listen to every call that Harold Wilson made or received. Haines thought this was such a waste of time and had it stopped at least for calls between him and the PM. Haines suggests in *Glimmers of Twilight* that Halls had become obsessed with his work and didn't know how to stop worrying about it.

At the beginning of 1970, when the election was fast approaching, Halls began to feel unwell and his wife urged him to see a doctor. She said later that she knew he was doing far too much, but he ignored her pleas and struggled on towards the general election, going on foreign trips with Wilson and still trying hard to oversee everything on the home front. On 3 April 1970, just nine weeks before the election, Michael Halls died of a heart attack. He was fifty-five.

Labour lost the election. Right up until polling day, they had been expected to win with the opinion pollsters predicting a comfortable majority. In fact, Edward Heath gained seventy-six seats and Labour lost seventy-five. The Tories ended up with an overall majority of thirty.

Once Labour was in opposition, Marjorie Halls, Michael's widow, began a campaign for damages, claiming her husband had died because of unusual strains put upon him by the relationship between Harold and Marcia. This caused panic in Harold Wilson and his team.

After thirty years have passed, all government documents can be made public as long as they don't damage state security. In 2002, correspondence between Mrs Halls and the civil service was published.

In one letter, written in 1972 by Mrs Halls to Sir William Armstrong, the head of the civil service, she said her husband had enjoyed his job until 1968 when Marcia Williams became pregnant by her lover Walter Terry, a journalist for the *Daily Mail*.

'The Prime Minister became so obsessed with the affairs of his personal political staff that it became increasingly difficult for Michael to get him to complete the essential work,' Mrs Halls wrote.

She alleged that Marcia had begun to harass Mr Halls into sorting out what he saw as trivial domestic problems, including the installation of a telephone in her new home.

Michael was extremely tired by the end of February 1970; Mrs Marcia Williams was moving house and causing even more trouble than usual – in a frenzy she even threatened, while on the telephone to me, that if certain matters concerning her house were not put right she would bring down the Prime Minister.

'You well know what she meant,' Mrs Halls wrote to Sir William, whom she had known personally for many years.

She mentioned that the only other people who knew this secret were her husband, the Prime Minister himself and Lord Goodman, Wilson's legal adviser.

Historians of the Wilson era have often wondered what gave Marcia Williams her enormous influence over the Prime Minister. The stress of dealing with what is described in the files as the 'bizarre atmosphere' of Wilson's Kitchen Cabinet cost Mr Halls his life, his widow wrote.

It is comparatively easy looking back now to see that Michael Halls felt the unusual nature of some of his work at No. 10 a huge burden. Brought up in the era when Prime Ministers were all powerful and women were there to serve them, he began to see Marcia as a demanding servant who was getting in the way of the real business of the men who were running the country. Some experienced civil servants and academic historians now believe Michael Halls just wasn't up to the heavy pressures of the job in Downing Street, and blaming Marcia and her demands were an important signal that he was under pressure and finding it hard to cope.

'He stayed later and later at the office to do the work that he should have been doing in normal hours, when he was distracted keeping the peace between various factions in No. 10,' his widow said.

The upsets between Mr Wilson and Mrs Marcia Williams increased until they reached a nightmarish climax in March 1970. He was so physically tired from the long hours he had to spend trying to get through the work against the background of the time-consuming H. Wilson–M. Williams upsets, that he confided to me at the time that he was no longer able to walk upstairs to the PM's study, but had to take the lift.

During those few weeks before he died, I pleaded with Michael to go and see a doctor, but he said the simple truth was that he could not find the time, so he went on screwing up the last ounce of his energy and life. Had he been able to rest during this period he would have stood a chance of survival.

But Sir William and Lord Jellicoe, then the minister in charge of the civil service, offered their regrets that they could not do anything for Mrs Halls because there was no medical evidence that stress could cause heart attacks.

Mrs Halls also wrote personally to Prime Minister Edward Heath, saying that there were 'facts in my case which I would rather not put into writing and which will not appear on the file'.

At the top of a memo from his principal private secretary, Heath wrote: 'We must help if we can.'

It was floated that it might be possible to top up Mrs Halls widow's pension with funds from secret sources such as the 'Special Services Fund' or something called the 'Fund for the Relief of Sundry Female Objects in Distress'.

When it became clear that information was reaching the press, those involved decided to bring Wilson in on the affair.

Heath told the Leader of the Opposition that he was prepared to see Mrs Halls, which Armstrong noted had an immediate and galvanising effect on the Labour leader.

> Mr Wilson thought it neither necessary nor desirable; there was a danger that, if she came to see the PM, she would 'pour the whole thing out' at him, and there was no need for him to subject himself to that, particularly if he was proceeding in the generous way he had in mind.

Even after this, Mr Heath said he was prepared to interview Mrs Halls but his principal private secretary dissuaded him:

> If Mrs Halls comes to see you, she will certainly take the opportunity of saying to you a number of things about her husband's term of office here, which will deal in detail and to Mr Wilson's discredit with his relations with his personal political secretary [Marcia] and possibly other members of his office.
>
> When you saw Mr Wilson, you said that you would be willing to see Mrs Halls, and I noticed that he was very quick to say that he thought you should not do so.

If he comes to know that you have seen Mrs Halls, he will think that you have deliberately disregarded what he said to you, and may think that you have done so in the hope of discovering information to his discredit.

Soon after, Mrs Halls threatened to sue the civil service. Lord Goodman, who had earlier suggested a pay-off, highlighted that no money could now be offered because it would look like Wilson was succumbing to blackmail.

Mrs Halls served her writ seeking £50,000 damages during the February 1974 election campaign. It received no publicity. Labour scraped back into No. 10 and there was no chance of a settlement once Wilson was in charge and taking a close personal interest in the case.

Mrs Halls was worn down by the legal delaying methods of the Treasury solicitor and the case simply faded away with no money being paid.

The story about Michael Halls's death and his wife's claim that having to deal with the personal relationship between Harold and Marcia had contributed to the overwork and emotional strain which had killed him first appeared in *Private Eye*. Two full-page pieces in consecutive editions – 'Mrs Williams's Dowry' and 'See Saw Marjorie Poor' – revealed the affair with Walter Terry, the births of Daniel and Timothy, the death of Michael Halls and the increasingly emotional relationships between Harold and Marcia, the Kitchen Cabinet and everyone who worked in Downing Street.

Mrs Halls had reported that just before he died, her husband had said to the Prime Minister that four years of working with Marcia was all he could take, and Harold Wilson had pointed out that he had put up with fourteen.

So, did Marcia ringing up and asking that her telephone be fixed kill Michael Halls? Professor Jon Davis reflects:

Competent officials don't agree to everything. The real key was that it was Wilson who damaged Halls by overpromoting him. That particular role then as now was known as one of the hardest in Whitehall. It was an immense administration role. Very hard to have somebody gentle and not so tough doing the job that Harold Wilson demanded of Michael Halls. He couldn't do it. It is the toughest job in the world and he wasn't up to it.

It's a temperament thing. In that job there is no concept of a work–life balance. And everyone knows whoever does that job, what that job is. It gives you kudos to succeed in that job, but it's no good if you are not up to it.

From what I understand, consensus opinion would be to blame Wilson, who put the wrong man in the wrong job.

In 1970, when Roy Jenkins was about to become deputy leader of the Labour Party, Harold Wilson felt Jenkins had to be told about the existence of Marcia's two sons, so he explained the situation to Joe Haines, because he didn't want to tell Jenkins himself. Presumably, Wilson guessed that if he told Jenkins that Marcia had two sons, he would assume that Wilson was the father. Haines was profoundly shocked by the news given to him by the Prime Minister. 'It would be trite to say I was astonished, and the understatement of the decade.'

13

Weddings and Disappearing Passports

Of all the strange tales about the goings-on of Marcia Williams, the events surrounding the marriage of her brother geologist Tony Field to Margarete Hutchinson, secretary to Sir Joseph Kagan, is one of the most bizarre.

The wedding happened in Barkisland, a picturesque Pennine hilltop village in Calderdale, West Yorkshire, where open moorland surrounds the local stone cottages and one very grand house: seventeenth-century Barkisland Hall. In addition, there's a school, a post office, two pubs, a cricket club and Christ Church Barkisland, a small and beautiful 1839 addition.

During that brief and unique period when Liz Truss was Prime Minister, I visited the church to research the story of the wedding. I went to a Sunday service at 11 a.m., where there were thirteen locals, the vicar and me. Time moves slowly in this part of the world. Two of the parishioners told me they had attended Tony and Margarete's wedding. One of them had been Margarete's Sunday school teacher.

The priest, Stephen Southgate, amazed me with a sermon on economics. He produced a plasticated flashcard from under his robe. '*OIKOS*' it said in large capitals. He explained that *oikos* is a Greek word which means economics and also household management. Thence followed an explanation of why trickle-down economics could never work. 'Blessed are the poor, but stuffing the mattress on the first floor would not cure suffering in the basement,' he said. The parishioners seemed unmoved. Maybe they'd heard it all before back in the 1970s.

On 16 June 1973, the Field family travelled from London to support Tony. Tony's dad had died recently so there were his two sisters, Peg and Marcia; Marcia's two sons, Timothy and Daniel; and Dorothy Matilda Falkender Field, widow of Harry and according to her story, often retold by Marcia, the illegitimate daughter of King Edward VII. Harold and Mary were also in attendance.

Tony was marrying Margarete Hutchinson, born in Barkisland less than a hundred yards from the church. Margarete was the secretary to Sir Joseph Kagan, the local millowner and owner of Barkisland Hall. The wedding happened just about the time I was attending Friday night soirées and big New Year's Eve parties at Barkisland Hall courtesy of Joe's growing friendliness with everyone at Yorkshire Television, including my husband.

When Tony married Margarete, he had been working unpaid for eighteen months as Harold Wilson's office manager. He even helped out as an unpaid driver at election time.

Joe Haines records the story of the wedding in *Glimmers of Twilight*, although this time he wasn't a witness to events but got the story when Harold Wilson phoned him at home late on the night of Tony's wedding.

Harold reported that Marcia and her children had flown to Leeds with his wife Mary and him in a private plane. Marcia had been upset because her boys had not been chosen to be pageboys at the wedding.

The bride recalls it wasn't like that at all. The boys weren't page-boys because no one outside the intimate circle of Harold, Marcia and their friends and workmates knew the boys existed. Everyone had spent huge amounts of time hiding a five- and a four-year-old from the British press and dispatching Harold Wilson's lawyer Lord Goodman to stop newspaper proprietors revealing all to their eager readers.

Margarete also said that Marcia's mum and the rest of the Field family were in on the cover-up, because Dorothy was ashamed to have a daughter who was an unmarried mother and saw it as a per-sonal tragedy for the family that there were two illegitimate grand-children. Margarete noted that it seemed like Dorothy was planning that their existence should go on being denied for ever.

Harold Wilson's driver Bill Housden said Marcia walked into the reception room, where the presents were on display in Barkisland Hall, and said to Tony, 'You have done very well here. You aren't going to get anything from me.'

Margarete remembers that Marcia was delayed back at Barkis-land Hall trying to find someone to keep an eye on her sons while she attended the wedding. Harold and Mary and the rest of the guests waited patiently for Marcia to appear in the church before the wedding could proceed.

As soon as the church ceremony was over, Marcia departed. Ac-cording to Joe Haines's version of events, she made her way back to Leeds Bradford Airport and demanded the waiting pilot fly her back to London. Presumably, the children went with her.

When she arrived at Heathrow, she had no passport nor any other proof of why she had commandeered the plane. Immigration officers asked who could vouch for her story and she explained that she worked for Harold Wilson, but in those pre-mobile phone days no one could confirm the story; Harold and Mary were incommunicado on their way back to London by train, having had their plane commandeered.

The bride and groom arrived in London en route for their honeymoon, and Tony went back to Marcia's house in Wyndham Mews, where he had been staying, to pick up their passports and tickets.

Everything was missing – tickets, passports, the lot. According to Joe Haines, Tony called the police who arrived just as Marcia reappeared from the airport. The story of the supposed burglary was retold and Marcia immediately produced the tickets and passports from a drawer where she said she had put them for safekeeping. I asked Margarete if this story was true and she sniffed and said Marcia had stuffed the tickets, passports and money under the kitchen sink.

14

Purple Hearts and Valium

On 28 February 1974, Harold Wilson and the Labour Party won the general election. They had a slightly lower share of the vote (37.2 per cent) than the Conservatives (37.9 per cent), but they won 301 seats. The Conservatives got 297 and the Liberals fourteen. Labour had no overall majority, so forming a government and running the country was going to be a tough time for everyone involved.

The pace inside Downing Street hotted up for all members of the Kitchen Cabinet, and it was at this moment in time that those two key chroniclers of the period, Bernard Donoughue and Joe Haines, began to record the increasingly eccentric behaviour of Marcia.

Joe had admired Marcia's political skills in the 1960s but he now noted that

the intemperate demands for Wilson to cancel whatever he was doing were appalling and too frequent: no one – wife, parent, sibling or secretary [all female roles back then] – who was wholly balanced should ever behave in such a fashion, but she did, to the distress of Wilson and the embarrassment of those around him.

Joe also reported in *Glimmers of Twilight* an afternoon in Marcia's office when she was raging on about a possible libel suit she wanted to take out against the *Evening Standard*. Joe suggested she should be careful because any QC employed by the paper might ask her difficult and embarrassing questions. 'Why?' she said. 'What could he ask me?'

Joe said he might ask about her children.

'Her face darkened as it always did when she was in a temper, and she exploded, "If he does that I shall destroy him" and she slapped her handbag.' Joe believes 'him' meant Wilson and not any QC hired by the *Evening Standard*.

Similarly, Bernard was beginning to note her agitation in his diaries. He wrote of a car journey he took with Marcia, where 'she sat agitatedly through the rest of the journey occasionally taking a pill of some kind'. These pills had also made an appearance four days before the election. On 24 February, Bernard had gone for lunch with Marcia, her sister Peggy and Joe Haines at St Ermin's Hotel. Bernard thought Marcia was depressed, as for the first time it had crossed her mind that they might lose the election. 'She took a purple heart earlier to keep awake, as she frequently does, and now has a headache,' he noted later. Despite her use of stimulants, Bernard said:

Her intelligence is undiminished. I can see why H. W. is fascinated with her ... This is not – now at least – a sexual relationship. Harold is astounded by her endless nervous energy, her instinctive capacity to go to the heart of any issue. He loves it when she shouts at him, corrects him, opposes him. It is the nearly incestuous father–daughter relationship with no mother and no guilt to intervene.

Around the same time, Albert Booth MP, a member of Wilson's Kitchen Cabinet, remarked casually to Bernard, 'She took her normal morning fistful of purple hearts before going out to lunch.'

Joe Haines added to the evidence:

There was another problem of which we were both aware. She wore a locket around her neck which contained tranquillisers prescribed by Joe Stone, Wilson's personal doctor, who had a deep loathing of her. Stone did not believe she could last for a long period under stress without recourse to the pills, which in the circumstances of a High Court action might not have been possible. He once said to me that if ever she appeared in court there would be a real risk of anything happening under cross examination, including her storming out of the witness box and the court precincts.

But I recognised Marcia's behaviour. Had she become addicted to her daily doses of purple hearts and tranquillisers?

Had the stress she had suffered since arriving in Downing Street, both from her job and from her extraordinary private life, plus the arrival of two babies ten months apart, made her like so many other women in the 1970s dependent on prescription drugs? Was Dr Stone like many family doctors of the period unaware that if he was prescribing her tranquillisers, he himself could be the cause of the dramatic change in her behaviour? I began collecting descriptions of the developing hysteria and eccentricity of Marcia's behaviour. In all the evidence supplied by Joe Haines and Bernard Donoughue, there were never any questions about what might have caused the dramatic changes in her behaviour. No one ever asked why she was behaving so strangely; her outbursts without exception were attributed to her passionate desire to 'control' Harold Wilson.

Life was already tough enough for Marcia and getting tougher. In 1974, it was unique for a woman with two small children, little money and no husband to be doing a key job as the Prime Minister's political adviser. Her son Timothy Williams was now six, and his brother Daniel five. Their father Walter Terry was still working as a lead political journalist on Fleet Street's most popular papers. After his second son was born to Marcia, he had returned home to his wife Mavis, described by Joe Haines as 'a lovely girl, smaller and much more attractive than Marcia'.

Marcia's dad had died in 1972 and she and her extended family – her mum, sister and two sons – were living in Wyndham Mews in a plum position near Oxford Street in central London. Once again Marcia was helped out with a deposit and mortgage support from Harold's generous Yorkshire friend Sir Joseph Kagan, with his secretary Margarete married to Marcia's brother being almost part of the extended Wilson–Field family.

Marcia was still Harold's right-hand woman, but she had become nervous and overworked and began to spend a lot of time working from home. She tried to keep in touch by phone, ringing and counselling and advising the Prime Minister at all hours of the day and night but with little thought or understanding for what he might have been doing at the other end of the line.

Repeatedly, he was dragged out of conferences or halted in the middle of an important speech to take a phone call from Marcia. That brought its own difficulties. She was tired and worried about money. Most of all she was terrified that the story of her two illegitimate sons which had been kept secret for years would be revealed by the press. But how could two small and lively lads be kept a secret for ever when their father was still a leading political journalist and their mother was the Prime Minister's political secretary? If there were journalists surrounding her house as she claimed every couple of days, how come they never took pictures or decided to spill the beans about Tim and Dan?

The answer was Arnold Goodman. Lord Goodman, as he became with a peerage from Harold Wilson in 1965, was a mighty lawyer with his own firm, Goodman Derrick. Everyone at Westminster and in the media, and particularly *Private Eye*, knew he was one of the most powerful men in Britain. If the newspapers weren't reporting the juicy story of the Prime Minister's closest adviser's illegitimate babies with a senior political journalist, then it would be because Lord Goodman himself had spoken to the proprietor of whatever newspaper was making the pitch this time and warned them off. When Arnold Goodman and a proprietor got together and discussed an important story, if Arnold decreed it, things just didn't happen.

Conjure up if you will a Twitter-free world, impossible in 2020 when a pregnant Carrie was living unmarried with Boris, her Prime Minister boyfriend, in Downing Street. In the late 1960s, people outside the Westminster bubble – and that would be most of the population of the UK – would have had no idea what was going on because no newspaper or television or radio station would have been allowed to report it. The power of newsmakers to supress gossip and news died with Arnold Goodman's generation and has been replaced with internet and social media and a rich mix of stories true and false, embroidered or exaggerated. The margins between real life and history have become fuzzy. Who knows when viewing *The Crown* where real life ends and the scenes imagined by the scriptwriter begin?

Back in 1974, when Labour won two elections and were back in power, whatever her other problems, Marcia believed with good reason that Harold would find it very tough to manage without her. She was his lightning connector to the real world. If she wasn't able to be constantly by his side watching over him, she was giving him instructions, often hysterically, by telephone. The private office and the Kitchen Cabinet had begun to notice now Harold was back in No. 10 that he often seemed weary and had begun to drink brandy much more frequently, and often late into the night. This had never been a problem in the 1960s. Marcia wanted to be watching over him, advising and protecting him, but her other personal problems weighed her down. As Joe Haines reports it, she was unpopular with her workmates who were delighted when she worked from home. The tension for Marcia became intolerable. She often insisted on telling Harold things urgently and at length, by telephone.

Night after night, Bernard wrote about her difficulties and the demands she placed on the Prime Minister and his inner circle. As the newest member of the team, Bernard – young, handsome and obliging – seemed to have been nominated by the Prime Minister as the man who could sort out Marcia's problems and protect her. As his diaries detail:

Monday April 1

Get a message to phone Marcia. I telephone. She is violent. Accuses me of conspiring to organise a lunch with H. W. and without her. Denounces everybody. I listen for half an hour then have to put the phone down.

Wednesday April 3

Day dominated by newspaper scandal stories about Marcia and land deals – involving letters with apparently forged signatures by H. W. Questions in the house. Calls for suspension of Marcia by Labour MPs.

Joe said the press could now go for Marcia and expose everything – her two illegitimate children, two houses, several personal domestic staff, all on four thousand pounds a year.

We sat around the Cabinet table, Joe, Albert and myself, discussing how to deal with it.

H. W. very angry and sad he turned to me and said, 'You should go and see Marcia. She has been with me 18 years, you have been here only a few weeks. She gets all this. Go and see her for only fifteen minutes. She really does like you.' He also asked me to write to her. His hatred of the press shone out.

The next day Marcia phoned Harold to tell him that the press were surrounding her house. Once again, the Prime Minister sent the trusty Bernard to remove them.

Gangs of seedy press louts and photographers were there blocking the road and the entrance to her house. They have been ringing the bell, beating on the door, pushing letters through and climbing on the windowsills and trying to look in and take photographs. We go in Marcia is in tears and totally destroyed. They have destroyed her. She is also angry with H. W. She says he has abandoned her and just looked after himself.

We went out to buy champagne and ice cream to cheer her up.

It was Harold Wilson who had advised Bernard Donoughue to keep a diary. When Bernard finally got round to publishing it thirty years later, many of the key Labour players in the 1970s had passed on. The pencilled notes scribbled nightly before he went to bed contained fascinating observations of Marcia. All the Prime Minister's inner circle seemed united in what they thought of her. There was absolute agreement that Marcia Williams was the most difficult woman any of them had ever met. Politics watchers, historians and journalists all asked just one question about Marcia's difficult behaviour from 1974 onwards. What was the hold she had over Harold that made her behave so badly? Everyone assumed without question that Marcia was a political dominatrix, hell-bent on governing Britain by keeping Harold Wilson firmly under her thumb.

To the young Bernard, it was fascinating. He and Joe Haines both reported regularly on her drug-taking habits without, it seems, any idea of how they could be affecting her behaviour.

Back in the 1960s and '70s, Britain was a rapidly changing place and drug taking had become common.

The 'purple hearts' which Marcia took frequently were a stimulant drug called Drinamyl by doctors and chemists but known as amphetamines, Benzedrine or speed to the young people who believed they stopped them getting fat, anxious or depressed. They were very easy to find in London in the 1970s, usually fetching about 1/6 for a tab from under the counter in cafes and bars – they were addictive and illegal. Marcia had begun to take them through the '60s Labour government. She was working extra-long hours without enough support staff and purple hearts kept her awake to get more work done.

The government were concerned about their rapidly growing use across Britain. In a contemporary investigation, it stated:

The abuse of amphetamine-barbiturate mixtures by doctor and patient has increased, is increasing and ought to be diminished. The Government has introduced the Drugs (Prevention of Misuse) Bill which is concerned with one aspect of this – the so-called 'purple heart' problem. Evidence has only recently become available that such a mixture really has effects different from those of its constituents taken singly. With 15mg of amphetamine and 300mg of cyclobarbitone psychic energy is increased, drowsiness is reduced and the human subject, if he resembles the rat, probably becomes less inhibited in social situations.

For people like Marcia who wanted to work long hours and stay awake, purple hearts were regarded as a godsend. They are no longer manufactured but played their part originally keeping soldiers alert and awake in battle. They won a footnote in history as the drug given to Prime Minister Anthony Eden when he suffered stomach pains during the Suez crisis. The story goes that he took purple hearts, his brain became confused and so did his policies.

As Marcia took more and more purple hearts to keep her awake and overstimulated, the effects became more and more obvious. Anxiety, loss of inhibition, hostility, aggressiveness and paranoia are all pointers to addiction to Drinamyl.

We don't know whether Marcia got her purple hearts from Dr Joseph Stone or a street dealer. She could well have been using them occasionally, or in smaller quantities and increasing her dosage over the years, but it appears that the combination of press pressure and a rising pile of personal problems built up over Wilson's first period in power seemed to be making her very unstable indeed.

Dr Stone took on the role of Marcia's medical adviser and pre-scriber because he saw it as a way of protecting Harold Wilson from her influence, which he believed was dangerous. He could see she was stressed and often 'hysterical'. There is little doubt that the prolonged heavy usage of the purple hearts, which were not only dangerously addictive but stripped away inhibitions, badly affected Marcia's ability to work with her colleagues.

Dr Stone, desperate to remove Marcia's influence over Harold, had begun prescribing tranquillisers 'to calm her down' and reverse the effect of the purple hearts. Stone told Joe Haines that Wilson could be Britain's greatest Prime Minister if only he, Joe Stone, could remove Marcia's influence. There was a pretty general agreement all round that this meant shutting her up or closing her down. Trying hard to do his job as the Prime Minister's doctor, Joe Stone was happy to supply Marcia with tranquillisers on demand. There cer-tainly didn't appear to be a shortage. When Percy Clark, a Labour Party official, was in tears after a row with a trade union, Marcia unscrewed the lid of the vial she wore round her neck and shook out a few to calm him down. Marcia had begun to take Valium prescribed by Dr Stone because he like so many other GPs of the period believed that they weren't addictive and that in her case they might soothe away her influence over the Prime Minister.

Joe Stone, like GPs across Britain, was handing them out to tired mums and stressed-out workers.

In 1966, the Rolling Stones came up with a hymn celebrating this newest form of tranquilliser and the rise in their dramatic overuse in Britain. Valium, Librium, Mogadon and Ativan were all benzodiazepines and dubbed 'Mother's Little Helper' by the Stones.

Valium and other benzodiazepines were hailed as wonder drugs. They were first manufactured by the American drug company Hoffmann-La Roche. Librium went on the market in 1960 and Valium in 1963. They appeared to be less toxic and less likely to cause dependence than older drugs. Medical professionals greeted them enthusiastically at first and they skyrocketed in popularity. At their peak in the mid to late 1970s, GPs in the UK wrote 30 million prescriptions for benzodiazepines. Joe Stone may well have believed that they were harmless and would negativise the effects of the purple hearts Marcia took, but the opposite proved to be true.

Like Marcia, I was a busy mum with two small kids and a taxing job as a producer/director with the BBC, Granada and then Thames Television, and I was taking steadily increasing doses of Valium every day. I had begun by going to my GP and telling him I felt stressed because I was busy with my children, my job and the part I had to play in my husband's role as an MP, and of course he prescribed Valium. The label said 2mg per day.

It was a great help for a very short time. I upped the dose and it seemed an even greater help, and then I started to feel a bit wobbly, to see myself as a nervous person, getting more anxious and stressed. It took me just a few weeks to realise I was hooked. Just like Marcia and pretty much everyone else in the media and Westminster, I drank alcohol every day. There was a bar in our office building and wine, beer and spirits were available with every meal in the Thames Television restaurant. Soon I was panicking every day; I couldn't and wouldn't leave the house without Valium in my handbag. I began having serious panic attacks, holding on to the walls of John Lewis in Oxford Street because the buildings appeared to be swaying. Trembling and shaking outside a supermarket while we were on holiday in Italy, I begged my husband to go in to buy some ham for the children's lunchtime sandwiches. I explained that the fluorescent lights were far too bright in Italian supermarkets, and I believed myself.

It wasn't hard to get Valium. Doctors more or less put it on repeat prescription and didn't ask too many questions. If I ran out of supplies, I explained that I was off on another overseas trip, and quickly I got what I wanted.

Addiction to benzodiazepines became an international scandal. By the time I went off to what was then Zimbabwe Rhodesia to film the arrival back in the capital of 'the Boys from the Bush' and Robert Mugabe, I was taking 20mg on very stressful days. As the people joyfully welcomed Mugabe in the middle of the recreation ground, I shook with terror in the same way Marcia is described as behaving. I thought I would be trampled to death as the crowd surged forwards and an angry journalist dragged me to safety.

A couple of months later, I was sent to New York to make a film with a female TV producer, Barbara Gordon, who had written a bestselling book about her own addiction to Valium, *I'm Dancing as Fast as I Can*. We interviewed Barbara at length and I listened to her describing the symptoms I myself was suffering.

Sensibly, I kept absolutely silent about my own recently discovered problems and used the opportunity to try to find out how to deal with my personal situation.

When we returned to the UK, I arranged for us to film an interview with Professor Malcolm Lader at King's College. Malcolm was Britain's leading expert on addiction to Valium. In 1978, he called benzodiazepines 'the opium of the masses' and said their use was 'the biggest medically induced problem of the late twentieth century'. He described the bizarre symptoms I knew so well:

> The brain is starting to wake up and it overwakes – sounds appear loud and lights appear bright, so they are wearing sunglasses indoors and they also have a symptom whereby they feel very unsteady and they will walk round the room holding on to the walls – and they really are then in a bad withdrawal state …
>
> It is more difficult to withdraw people from benzodiazepines than from heroin.

I started trying to sort my personal problem when *TV Eye* at Thames Television was off the air for the summer. With a strength I hadn't realised I possessed, it took me just over two years to give up Valium completely. Every day I reduced my dose by a tiny amount. Sometimes I regressed, but eventually the day came when I was brave enough to leave the house without Valium. It took years before I was brave enough to throw away my remaining supplies. I have never, however bad the day, taken one again.

In an attempt to help other addicts, I made several more programmes about tranquilliser addiction, and I realised when reading descriptions of Marcia's behaviour what it was that was likely making her behave so strangely. Not only was she taking Valium in generous quantities; she was mixing it with purple hearts.

Joe Stone, along with GPs across the land, may well have believed that Valium might calm Marcia down and reduce the effects of the purple hearts, but the opposite was the case.

Today, young people thinking of taking drugs can Google the consequences of mixing purple hearts and Valium:

> Combining Valium with a stimulant can significantly impact a person's brain chemistry. Valium can reduce one's heart rate while stimulants can increase it. When both drugs are combined, this could have a negative impact on the heart. Using both types of drugs simultaneously could also increase the risk of overdose.

One study looked at how using amphetamines and Valium together affected the heart. The study published in *Medical Hypotheses* determined that using the two together could potentially lead to myocardial ischemia, which is reduced blood flow to the heart.

So Marcia's situation was much worse than mine. In addition to probable tranquilliser addiction, she was taking purple hearts to keep her awake throughout the day because she felt so tired and weary from the Valium she was taking to calm her down. She is often described as shaking and pale by both Bernard and Joe.

They were both severely worried by her behaviour in 1974, really right from the start of their joint efforts to support Harold Wilson and his new government. If anyone guessed what Marcia's problem was, they certainly never said so. She was severely overworked, aiding the Prime Minister, running the political side of the premiership, bringing up two small boys alone and trying to protect the boys and herself from the revelation of their family situation and who their father was. Added to that, Marcia must have guessed that sooner or later the truth would be revealed to the world, not about her drug taking but her role as a single mum, still not accepted as a next-door neighbour let alone as the political secretary in 10 Downing Street.

Everyone who worked with Marcia thought her unacceptable behaviour, her fear and her hysterical reaction to the world around her happened because she was terrified of losing her grasp on Harold Wilson. But she was worrying every day that she was losing her grasp on everything, that she would not be able to cope with her children let alone her job with Harold.

Joe Stone was worried too, but I think he believed as did other GPs about their patients across the land that she needed more medication to help her survive. He explained to Joe Haines that Marcia would never be able to give evidence in a court case, that she needed watching and helping at every turn because he believed her extreme behaviour could destroy the Prime Minister.

Marcia Williams's behaviour changed dramatically during the Wilson governments of the 1960s. The civil servants whose job it was to work with and protect the Prime Minister had from the beginning in 1964 seen her as pushy, aggressive and opinionated, but that was to be expected. A young attractive woman appearing in a senior role in No. 10 in the 1960s was unique, so she was bound to be evaluated, criticised and teased by staff of both sexes. All agreed she was difficult and odd. Everyone questioned her right to be there, why had she crossed the boundaries of what was normal for women? Politics and government were most certainly not normal for women then. The people who 'ran things' were middle-aged white men whose most important role was preserving the status quo. Behind her back, they referred to Marcia as the 'office wife'. The name had spread from an early American talkie where a hopelessly devoted female secretary did everything and more for her boss at work than his wife managed to do at home.

There were plenty of female workers in Downing Street when Harold and Marcia arrived. Glamour was provided by the shorthand typists who did their duties in the basement rooms overlooking the garden. The Garden Room Girls were well-educated middle-class young women who'd been to private schools and then on to the best secretarial colleges. They claimed Marcia was bossy and assertive. She was a woman where women had never been before, extremely close to the Prime Minister. She gave out orders which had to be obeyed.

The civil servants had experienced problems in the past with various Prime Ministers' wives and mistresses but discovered they could be talked down to, and then ignored. They soon got bored with the serious business of government and went away. Marcia was different. She knew more about politics than the rest of the politicians put together, and she had clear ideas of her own about the way things should be done, stated them forcefully and achieved excellent results.

All this is much as you might expect sixty years ago, but once her sons were born in 1968 and '69 things got increasingly worse for Marcia. She was exhausted and she was often terrified. The burden of all her secrets was hard to bear and it could surely only be the overuse of the purple hearts to boost her capacity to work long hours and the Valium prescribed by Dr Stone to calm her down which caused her to change from a demanding woman into a tense and terrified extremist who more and more became hysterical when things were difficult or she failed to get what she wanted. Everyone in Downing Street talked about her, everyone complained about her, but it seems it didn't occur to anyone that she might be ill or need some help. It is important to remember that no one noticed that she was pregnant, not once but twice in Downing Street in the late '6os. We have to accept that Joe Haines and the male civil servants failed utterly to notice, but the female workers? Did they whisper and gossip at work but never say a word outside the building? Or did they believe that she was still handily married to an invisible Mr Williams somewhere in London?

Whatever the reasons for the silence about her pregnancies and deliveries, Marcia and her deteriorating behaviour at work was at the heart of three huge stories that exploded during the four years Ted Heath was occupying Downing Street and Labour was in opposition.

On 12 January 1972, Mary Wilson turned fifty-six. She and Harold had been married for thirty-two years. As a birthday treat, he arranged to take Mary out to lunch at L'Epicure, a famous French restaurant in Soho. Roy Jenkins was a frequent luncher there, so it would have been well known in posh Labour Party circles as an alternative to the Gay Hussar, the Hungarian restaurant more famous for its left-wing diners and plotters than family celebrations. When my husband Austin Mitchell became an MP in 1977, we started visiting the Gay Hussar, always packed with politicians and trade unionists flattered by the attention they got from the owner, Victor Sassie. When politicians visited from my native New Zealand, we took them to the Gay Hussar so they could spot celebrities of the left. It closed in 2018, by which time L'Epicure had been gone for decades.

L'Epicure was one of the top showbusiness restaurants in London in the 1970s, distinguished by a flaming gas torch above the front door whenever the restaurant was open. Actors and their agents would lunch on potted shrimps; elderly waiters would sail their trolleys across the wavy-patterned carpet, offering steaks to be cooked at your table and crêpes Suzette to be set on fire in front of you. Perhaps all the theatrical activity made it a good place to take your wife to lunch if you didn't have too much to talk about.

Joe Haines in *Glimmers of Twilight* described what happened as an appalling episode 'almost too dreadful to comprehend'. Until that fatal day, his relationship with Marcia had been very good. He admired her skill and he credited her fairly as an important reason why Labour was victorious in the elections of 1964 and '66. But he had noticed a huge change in her behaviour. 'Greed, jealousy and uncontrolled rages had for some time been eating into her previously acute political perception,' he wrote.

In the early evening of 12 January, Harold Wilson came back from a visit to his home in Lord North Street and asked to have a private word with Joe Haines. Joe said Harold was tense and somewhat embarrassed. Marcia had been working from home that day, as she did a great deal of the time after the birth of her sons, and one of the Garden Room Girls had telephoned her to let her know that Harold was taking Mary to lunch for her birthday. Marcia had apparently exploded in rage, and when Mary got back home after lunch, Marcia had telephoned her and announced that she wanted to see her immediately. Mary set out alone for Marcia's home in

Wyndham Mews on the north side of Oxford Street. When Mary arrived, Marcia came to the door and said, 'I have only one thing to say to you. I went to bed with your husband six times in 1956 and it wasn't satisfactory.'

There is no record of what Mary did, but perhaps, with a calmness she was renowned for, she said nothing at all and made her way back to Lord North Street, called Harold and asked him to come home.

Joe says Harold managed to convince his wife that Marcia was just being hysterical and jealous, and Mary had believed him, but at the end of his conversation with Joe, Harold's face had brightened and he said, 'Well, she has dropped her atomic bomb at last. She can't hurt me any more.'

No one will ever know what really happened between Harold and Marcia when they first came together in 1956. Both of them, throughout their lives, gave several different versions of what happened. That's easy to understand. All of us looking back romanticise some of the stories in our past, big up others and wipe the slate clean when we could only be embarrassed if the truth came out. It's hard to believe Marcia had suddenly decided to invent an affair to punish Harold and Mary nearly two decades later, particularly when she was telling the story of an unsuccessful sexual relationship. Probably, she was telling the truth, however unacceptable it was to all of them. Maybe George Caunt in his unpublished and gossipy papers about Marcia and Harold's behaviour back in the 1950s was right. Had Marcia got pregnant and had an illegal abortion when she was working at Montague L. Meyer? Was that the 'bombshell' to which Harold referred? Surely a bit of unproveable unsuccessful sex twenty years earlier is hardly worthy of that description?

There was no doubt Marcia loved and admired Harold, loved the success that came from their joint efforts and loved the many achievements of those 1960s Labour governments, but she was bitterly sad at the way things had turned out. She was terrified the story of her now finished affair with Walter Terry and the arrival of the little boys would be revealed. Her father had recently died, her mother was now living with her in Wyndham Mews, she was nearly forty years old without any prospect of ever marrying again and it seemed unlikely to her then that Harold would ever be Prime Minister again. She now had two sons to bring up alone, little money and the prospect of a whole working lifetime to come to support her family. Marcia's sister-in-law Margarete Field said to me that Marcia wouldn't have minded if people thought Tim and Dan were Harold's sons, and indeed when they finally made their appearance in *Private Eye* there were many people who may well have believed that.

15

Fields of Slag and Gold

Harold and Marcia had become intimate friends from the day
they met in 1956 and they stayed that way for the rest of their
lives. Their two families seemed intertwined, much closer than
those of many married couples who don't see one another from one
year's end to the next. There were long periods when all the Wilsons
and all the Fields were working together and, if not living together, had houses within a few miles of each other and spent off-duty
weekends together. However Marcia and Harold's relationship had
begun, it turned out to be permanent. There was always gossip and
speculation about how they got on together, and whether it was
true or false, it was hard for Marcia to bear. For a woman who had
made Labour politics and governing the country her main aim and
ambition, it was disheartening that her private life and her closeness
with Harold was still a major fascination for her workmates and the
journalists whose job it was to report politics in action. But it did
seem to matter greatly to Marcia that her family should be closely
involved with her work. By the time Harold became Prime Minister for the third time in February 1974, every member of the Field
family had strong relationships with Downing Street.

Marcia's elder sister Peg lived with Marcia, their mum and Marcia's sons Tim and Dan in Wyndham Mews. For a time, Peg worked as secretary to Mary Wilson, answering mail and fixing engagements for the Prime Minister's wife. She was awarded an MBE for her work in Harold Wilson's resignation honours list.

Marcia and Peg's brother Tony Field, a skilled geologist who had worked in the Middle East for the Iraq Petroleum Company, was encouraged by Marcia to return to Britain to join Harold's support gang. At election time, he worked as Harold's driver and when Labour lost the 1970 election, he then spent a couple of years as office manager for Harold as the Leader of the Opposition. Tony was working for the Bath and Portland Stone Group at the same time, so was able to work for Harold Wilson without payment.

As with all Harold's staff, once you were in, you were a friend as well as an employee; the boundaries between different roles often melted away. During the time Tony was Harold's office manager, the Troubles were becoming a serious problem in Northern Ireland and Tony was invited on a trip with Harold, Merlyn Rees MP and Joe Haines to meet some 'friends of the IRA'.

Dr John O'Connell, in his memoirs, recalls how in March 1972 he was approached by Irish Republican leaders to act as a go-between with Harold Wilson, then Leader of the Opposition. O'Connell, a Labour MP in Dublin, travelled to London to give Wilson a document setting out IRA proposals for a ceasefire. On 13 March, Wilson met O'Connell in Dublin's Shelbourne Hotel. O'Connell took Wilson to a rendezvous, where the IRA leaders were already sitting at a long table. Wilson, accompanied by Merlyn Rees, Joe Haines and Tony Field, sat at the other end of the table facing David O'Connell, Joe Cahill and John Kelly. Nothing came of the meeting, but it demonstrates how trusting Harold was of those he had become close to. Tony Field was now and for ever a bona fide member of the Labour leader's inner circle.

But it was the work Tony was doing when he was not working unpaid for Harold that was about to become very newsworthy indeed and make him a national figure.

When Tony first came back to the UK in 1967, he got a job as quarry manager for Bath and Portland Stone. He suggested the company buy a quarry enhanced by heaps of slag from the coal mining industry at Ince-in-Makerfield near Wigan. The 'Wigan Alps' to local residents. Bath and Portland ignored his advice, so Tony set up on his own and bought the thirty-acre site for £27,281. His widow Margarete explained to me that Tony worked day and night to remove the slag and sold much of it to the builders of the M62 motorway. It now forms the heavy-duty underlay to the ribbon of tarmac which links the east coast of England with the west, from the outskirts of Liverpool to Hull via Manchester and Leeds. Just after Tony had sold his slag to the motorway builders, the local Ince Council granted planning permission for the now empty site to be used as an industrial estate, so in 1973 Tony moved on from quarries and slagheaps to property speculation, taking his mum along as co-director and Peg and Marcia as sleeping partners in a second company. Tony really was worried and conscientious about his unmarried sisters, one with two small children to bring up, and he had promised his father he would look after them. In those days, unmarried women were still often seen as their father's dependents. Tony took on some of what might have been his dad's responsibilities for Marcia and Peg, and they became co-owners of his reclamation company. No member of the Field family did anything illegal.

They hoped they would make a bankable profit by selling the now slag-free land.

But on 18 March 1974, sandwiched between the two elections Harold and Marcia won for the Labour Party that year, the *Daily Mail* headlined an exclusive article about a man called Ronald Milhench: 'The case of Ronald Milhench and his £950,000 land deals'. It certainly was a huge scoop which remained in the headlines for weeks.

Milhench, who was aged thirty-two and from Wolverhampton, claimed he was a wealthy insurance broker. He was appearing just weeks after an incident in which a hire car he was driving ran into the water at Chasewater Lake, Cannock, drowning his 27-year-old wife Kathleen, a singer with the Salvation Army pop group. Milhench had recently doubled his payments on a life insurance policy on Kathleen. An inquest jury had returned a majority verdict of accidental death. Milhench explained to the coroner that grouped together, his business interests were worth more than £500,000. One of his commitments was payment for thirty-four acres of land at Ince-in-Makerfield in Lancashire, which the *Mail* described as an unlovely place, and which Milhench had bought from Tony Field. He was committed to paying for another sixty-one acres.

By the time Milhench appeared before the court, Tony had owned the land for seven years and completely cleared the site. He had worked hard and was absolutely entitled to sell it. The *Mail* helpfully published a photograph of the ownership documents for the land. Tony Field had two partners, his sisters Peggy Field and Marcia Williams. Marcia's occupation was political secretary to the Prime Minister. The *Daily Mail* had a Field day. The press set up an almost permanent base camp outside Marcia's house.

Barely a week before this story broke, in the Queen's speech following the first 1974 election, Prime Minister Harold Wilson and his Labour government had committed themselves to taking all development land into public ownership, so the idea that the Field family, all Downing Street trusties, might make fat profits out of the sale of land to Milhench was seen as a total scandal. Tony, who had done nothing illegal, explained publicly that all he was trying to do was give his poor unmarried sisters some financial security, but the press didn't see it that way. Harold Wilson, always loyal to his friends, refused to take the advice of his ministers, his civil servants and Joe Haines and Bernard Donoughue and got up in the House of Commons and defended the Fields.

The Prime Minister said:

Mr Field worked in the office of the Leader of the Opposition for two years until June 1973 as office manager on a part-time basis. He drew no salary ...

I knew that in 1967 – four years before he joined my office – Mr Field has formed a family business, involving his father, a former small builder and other members of the family. On occasion he discussed the slag clearance transaction with me. The precise details were none of my concern, though it was clearly an enterprising transaction which would have the effect of retrieving unusable land for desirable uses. But I did, of course, know that Mr Field had been actively engaged working on the site, and, as any regular golf partner would be able to discover, that he broke his leg in an industrial accident there.

Then Harold went on to defend Marcia:

Much press reference has been made to Mr Field's sister, Mrs Williams, who has been my political and private secretary for many years, though not a civil servant at any time. Many of my right hon. and hon. friends, and indeed some other honourable members, know her and would pay tribute to her loyalty to our party and her contribution to the political life of this present generation. For several days now she has been subject to an intolerable degree of newspaper harassment on her doorstep, including an unauthorised entry into her car, and the incitement of children to hammer upon her door.

Bernard Donoughue described it all in his diary: 'The press behave appallingly, sitting and standing on the windowsill, trying to see through the windows and bribing boys to bang on the door, ring the bell and shout obscenities through the letter box about H. W. and Marcia.'

Bernard, Marcia and Joe Haines then went off to see the lawyers. 'Marcia was in good form, highly tranquillised,' wrote Bernard. Writs were duly issued against various papers. When the trio got back to Wyndham Mews, Terry Lancaster of the *Mirror* was there. 'We had champagne again,' wrote Bernard,

then heard the bad news from Walter Terry who works for the *Express*, that the *Express* was going to run the story of Marcia's two children – of which he is the father. Marcia collapsed in tears, we desperately tried to get in touch with H. W. who was in a car going to Oxford. The police were sent to intercept.

Eventually, Bernard went home late for a dinner party with several guests including journalists. 'Harold phoned in the middle of the hors d'oeuvres. He was in a telephone booth at the Oxford Labour Club, with people milling round and he kept shouting at them to "close the bloody door", Bernard noted.

Harold explained to Bernard that Marcia was in a desperate position, and that Bernard must go round to her house immediately and pull the telephone wires from the walls to stop her speaking to the press. Loyal Bernard once again departed his dinner party guests to be met with good news on his return to Wyndham Mews. Arnold Goodman had got hold of the editor of the *Daily Express* and stopped him publishing the exciting story that Marcia Williams, right-hand woman to the Prime Minister, had two children by his own political editor.

In *Tell Them I'm on My Way*, the memoirs of Lord Goodman published by Chapmans in 1993, Lord Goodman told the story with important differences. He said that Joe Haines had called him at home and begged him to ask Max Aitken to stop the *Express* from publishing the story about Marcia's boys.

I demurred, pointing out to Haines that as the chairman of the Newspaper Publishers Association I had to be very careful to avoid interfering with press stories in any way. But he urged on me that it was the Prime Minister's particular wish that I should do anything I could to prevent publication. I am afraid, rather weakly, I said that I would speak to Max ... Max's reaction was very satisfactory. 'I do not think we are under any duty to publish malicious gossip,' he said, 'which remains gossip however true it may be.' He indicated that he would telephone the editor and direct him not to publish anything. I telephoned Haines to tell him of my success and to urge upon him necessity for extreme discretion … Haines assured me that everything at his end would remain secret, but a few years later I was both surprised and vexed to find that he had retailed the story in his memoirs without any indication of his pledge of confidentiality.

Back at Marcia's home, Bernard reported that Peggy and Marcia were exhausted by events, so they were sent upstairs to get some rest. He went home to make a third attempt at his evening meal. The dinner party was still in full swing.

By the time he sat down to write in his diary about the day's events, Bernard was full of sympathy for Marcia.

How can one abandon her before these vermin? I am not a friend in any true sense, but she needs them now and I am a reasonable substitute. Certainly I could not abandon her now. Actually the business about exposing her young children to such pain shook me and I could easily have killed the journalist – like treading on a louse.

In the House of Commons, Harold Wilson commented:

These activities, if I may use so neutral a word to describe them, would, I am sure, offend the vast majority of journalists, all of whose names are blackened by them. Members on this side of the House might reasonably conclude that, although she has been the principal victim of this behaviour, this is a cowardly way of attacking me, which is the purpose, and, through me, the government.

Of course, the Prime Minister was right. Marcia was being tormented because of her intimate relationship with him and her important role as his political adviser. Until proved otherwise, there was always the strongly held belief that Marcia had some unbreakable hold on Harold Wilson, and if detractors persecuted her long and hard enough, they could destroy her and, through her, him and the Labour government.

Harold did the right thing, he stood up and supported Marcia loudly and clearly, but Britain was in transition from being a country where the Establishment, the men at the top and their wives and lovers, were still in control of what got published in the papers. Harold Wilson's lawyer Arnold Goodman and other powerful lawyers were able to threaten newspaper proprietors effectively with writs for libel, and time after time the publication of stories about Marcia, her lover and their sons was withdrawn just before papers went to press.

Private Eye doggedly went on reporting facts to their readers, the Establishment, the journalists and youthful truth seekers who were angry that the privilege of secrecy was still available to the men at the top.

Harold Wilson continued to defend Marcia relentlessly:

It is right that I should say straight away that Mrs Williams played no part whatsoever in the running of the company involved in the slag clearance operation and never had any dealings, business or social, with any of the property men described in the various press reports ...

While I have always drawn a distinction in my public speeches before and during the election between property development and land speculation, I believe – and we are committed to this – that the only way to deal with these problems is for all land required for development and redevelopment to come into public ownership. On this we are urgently engaged, and the more that I have read in the past week, the more urgent I think it is ...

Sir, I have tried to set out in some detail the issues raised by the stories and allegations which have appeared in the media. I hope I have made clear that there is no justification whatever in the attempts that have been made to sensationalise the affair and no reason why any member of my own staff should forfeit the trust I place in them.

But that wasn't the end of the affair. The following week, Milhench produced a letter on House of Commons paper signed by Harold Wilson which seemed to show that the Prime Minister himself was involved in Tony Field's land development deals. The letter apparently signed by Wilson was shown by Milhench to a *Daily Mail* reporter. It was dated 16 March 1973.

'Tony and I feel sure you are quite capable of carrying our Ince-in-Makerfield through with efficiency and discretion,' said the letter nonsensically. Milhench had produced it in an attempt to prove he was a credit-worthy person of good character. It had the opposite effect when it was quickly discovered that Harold Wilson's signature was forged. Milhench was described at his trial as a man whose vanity and ambition far outreached his intelligence and financial resources.

The journalists who felt robbed of their long-awaited scoop about Marcia and her boys continued their investigation into the Field family's affairs and stepped up their 24-hour vigil outside Marcia's home. For Tony Field and the sisters he was trying to protect, the situation was disastrous. Tony had prepared a package of land suitable as an industrial site. He had sold the slagheap site for £10,000 an acre, producing a profit of more than £200,000. But then he joined up with a property developer to buy a four-acre site next door and sold it to the highly dubious Milhench. The Field family then paid £131,000 for a third adjoining site of sixty-one acres. This purchase had not been completed by the time the story was spread across the front pages of all the papers, and the sale fell through.

On 24 June 1975, Bernard Donoughue wrote in his diary:

I received a transcript of the Milhench trial today. One interesting point emerges: he did pay Tony Field's company, in which Marcia and Peggy have a stake, £340,000. So they may have made a huge profit. The problem is apparently that they used the money to buy more land which they now cannot sell.

Harold Wilson was untouched by the scandal of the land deals affair. Once it was discovered that Milhench was a crook who was sent to prison, all the odium and scandal fell even more heavily at Marcia's front door.

Joe Haines complained about what he believed to be Marcia's role in it all – taking Harold's eye off the ball and demanding attention.

It was all a dreadful distraction from our main task, the country was in crisis with fears of inflation rising to banana republic levels and presided over by a Prime Minister and Cabinet which lacked a majority in Parliament. Every waking hour ought to have been devoted to helping the Prime Minister in every possible way to master the situation. Instead of that, day after day we were stuck with the difficulties afflicting his personal secretary and her family.

Wilson, engaged day and night in trying to cope with an economic and industrial crisis such as Britain had never known in peace time, a Prime Minister who had won more general elections than any man since Gladstone and to whom the country had given its trust, was once again being worn down by the increasingly demanding and hysterical calls upon his time and his emotions by a woman of no elected position who publicly never claimed to be more than his personal and political secretary.

The fact that Marcia was Harold's closest confidante, the person who had been with him and supported him and had been his political partner since long before he won his first election as party leader, meant nothing to Joe Haines. He failed utterly to understand the relationship between Harold and Marcia.

Harold Wilson was a decent man who had always been completely loyal to his friends and colleagues and most of all to Marcia, and he believed that what had happened to her and her family was tragic and unfair.

Just a couple of months later, after he had beaten back the press over the Milhench affair, Harold mentioned to Barbara Castle that something was going to happen soon that she wasn't going to like. She tried to tease the story out of him but failed.

Furious about the way Marcia had been treated, the Prime Minister raised two fingers to the press and her detractors. It was announced on 11 July in the *London Gazette*:

The Queen has been pleased by Letters Patent under the Great Seal of the Realm, bearing date the 11th day of July 1974, to confer the dignity of a Barony of the United Kingdom for life upon Marcia Matilda Falkender (formerly Marcia Matilda Mrs Williams), CBE, by the name, style and title of BARONESS FALKENDER, of West Haddon in Northamptonshire.

Barbara Castle wrote in her diary:

The papers are full of Marcia's installation in the Lords yesterday, which I did not get time to go and see. Ted [Barbara's husband] tells me she did it impeccably and with dignity. Whatever else one thinks of her she certainly is a remarkable personality. Personally I always got on well with her, but it is astonishing how many people are outraged at Harold's gesture – including Mik [Ian Mikardo]. It is typical of Harold that he should have gone to watch his own handiwork. The cheeky chappie is also the stubborn one. But Ted says their Lordships are disgusted by *The Times* for its profile of Marcia today, revealing that she has two children by Walter Terry. So dog has at last eaten dog! But the hack journalists of the right-wing press must be desperate in their determination to discredit Harold if possible.

Some people, including Joe Haines, although he produces no proof, believed that Marcia forced or cajoled Wilson to make her a peer.

'Though it was Wilson's proposal in the formal sense, he was merely endorsing Marcia's demands. When he announced the peerage to us, the thump of our hearts hitting our boots must have been heard in Outer Mongolia,' Haines wrote. He suggested that he and others in the Kitchen Cabinet tried to stop the Prime Minister from going ahead with the idea.

When Lady Falkender took her seat in the House of Lords on 23 July 1974, the press felt they had been silent long enough. The newspapers were not aware of many of the things that happened behind closed doors, the things which worried Joe Haines and upset the young Bernard Donoughue, but *The Times* certainly believed that the award of a peerage to the Labour Prime Minister's secretary must surely be wrong, especially so soon after Labour's re-election.

A huge profile, an appropriate size for the obituary of an American President, ran over two separate days and showed clearly how angry the press were that they had been forced to cover up Marcia's private life for so long.

'From a secretary's chair to a seat in the House of Lords' sang the first day's headline, spread across five columns. The article noted that while Marcia's life peerage was a reward for years of 'loyal devotion', the timing of the announcement led some to think it was 'an act of defiance to all those who have questioned her power and position, and a reply to the publicity that surrounded Mrs Williams and her family over the land deals affair'.

The journalist Caroline Moorehead went on to point out that although Marcia might have gathered a few friends along the way for being 'kind, sympathetic and immensely shrewd', she had also amassed a solid phalanx of enemies in her years at Transport House, in the opposition leader's room in the House of Commons and in No. 10 Downing Street. Such enemies felt that 'she is a highly strung woman of prejudices, and that her presence by Mr Wilson's side has tended to isolate him from the main course of Labour Party politics'.

Strong stuff, even Boris Johnson at the peak of press opprobrium didn't get such tough treatment, but it's hard to think what the male equivalent of 'a highly strung woman of prejudices' could be.

But the revelations about Marcia were building to a climax. Her defensiveness and refusal to participate in interviews shrouded her in an air of mystery and did little to combat growing rumours about her influence. An anonymous election adviser said he believed Marcia was the most important person in Britain after her boss. Harold had 'made her an object of public inquiry' by granting her the peerage at this time.

The Times then discussed the much delayed revelations about Baroness Falkender's private life and her two sons, revealed recently by *Private Eye*, which the *New Statesman* had berated for 'prurient curiosity'. *The Times* explained that Marcia had somehow managed to hide the fact that she had twice become a mother in ten months from all those who worked with her every day in Downing Street. One Downing Street staffer was quoted as saying, 'We thought she had had bad health; she used to come in to the office usually in the evenings.'

This was followed by breathless admiration of her remarkable stamina, revealing that she works far into most nights, never leaving the office until she has cleared every last piece of paper from her desk.

The Times pointed out how much time Harold and Marcia spent together. They lunched together, often with Mary Wilson, and saw each other most days, speaking on the telephone on the rare days they didn't cross paths. It was clear the Prime Minister valued Marcia's contributions and opinions very highly indeed.

There were never accusations that Marcia didn't do her work properly or that she was anything less than super-efficient. But the reality was always the same: there had never been a woman of such authority in Downing Street before. What did her 'hold' over the Prime Minister mean?

The paper came up with some examples of how she dominated her boss:

> She is said to have argued with him continually over Rhodesia. 'You can wheel and deal but there really are limits,' she told him then. 'You're going too far.' She also stopped him being too jokey on television at the last election. 'We don't want Harold the co-median,' she told the organisers. She is very concerned about his image. An apocryphal story is told about how when an impor-tant visitor called at No. 10 and asked to see her, he was told: 'I'm sorry. Mrs Williams is very busy, but the Prime Minister can see you now.'

Certainly, the extent to which she controlled access to the Prime Minister is something that enraged and upset many people, par-ticularly civil servants. They noted that Harold was elected to his job and Marcia was an employee, so such control was unusual. Joe Haines and Bernard Donoughue both highlighted a huge amount of screaming and shouting which made life unpleasant for Marcia's co-workers. Joe and Bernard felt they were forced to spend far too much time sorting out the peace and calming down the troops. There's no doubt that Marcia made trouble. She wasn't good enough at handling relations with her workmates, and they weren't good enough at handling her. It is easy to see looking back that she was a frontierswoman when it came to men and women sharing power. Neither side knew how to deal with a new situation where rules had yet to be made for men and women to work together on an equal footing. Men were still wearing hats and doffing them when they met a woman they knew. Men were still opening doors for women, and standing up for them on public transport. Most women were still doing the 'heavy lifting' when it came to running their households and bringing up children and they were still responsible for all the cooking, shopping and housework. You didn't have to be a feminist or a woman's libber to see that. Harold Wilson and Marcia Williams's period in Downing Street was the beginning of fifty years of enormous social change.

Much of Marcia's influence seems to come from her extreme sensitivity to people's attitudes, determining not only whether they are 'loyal' to the Prime Minister (a quality she seems to rate above all others) but just how far they can be trusted. 'She kept in touch with the people who would give him the right support,' says one friend of many years' standing. At times, this insecurity about people's motives has been excessive. She is said, for instance, to have had a definite say in the timing of the 1970 election, and in the American-style walkabouts of Harold Wilson's campaign. Prime Ministers are isolated people, and the value of a loyal confidante who is always there, who is perceptive and totally unsycophantic, should not be underrated. 'Harold Wilson is a shrewd operator in politics, and he has been lucky in having one of the shrewdest political assistants around,' says a close colleague.

16

Marcia and Harold Back in Power

The year of 1974 was a tense one indeed for British politics, with two general elections being held. In the February election, Labour were the largest party and gained fourteen seats, but they were still seventeen seats short of an overall majority, resulting in a hung parliament for the first time since 1929. So Labour held a second election in October and succeeded in getting a majority over all other parties, but it was tiny. Just three seats.

Harold Wilson was back at the top with his right-hand woman Marcia, but they had only eighteen months left of running the show. There had been a great many revelations about Marcia over the past decade, including about her secret sons, and things had become very tough for her indeed.

But with the boys' public presence and the stress that this caused Marcia came further allegations of her volatile behaviour. To understand these accounts from someone who worked with her following the 1974 election victory, I spoke to Lord Butler of Brockwell, the most distinguished civil servant of his generation. He was private secretary to five Prime Ministers – Heath, Wilson, Thatcher, Major and Blair – Cabinet Secretary and then head of the civil service for a decade, as well as master of University College, Oxford, and the head of the Review of Weapons of Mass Destruction Inquiry. Yet his amazing career nearly exploded when Marcia and Harold arrived in Downing Street.

In 1972, 34-year-old Robin Butler had arrived in Downing Street as a junior private secretary on a three-year secondment from the Treasury:

I came in when Heath was Prime Minister to do the MPs' correspondence and the briefings for MPs and Prime Minister's Questions, then half-way through I moved over to the Treasury desk and economic affairs and economic speeches. And, of course, there was the Miners' Strike.

When Harold Wilson won the election in February 1974, I became even more involved with the Miners' Strike. Robert Armstrong was the principal private secretary. He dealt with anything really important, with intelligence and appointments and that sort of thing, and I did the run-of-the-mill economic stuff including writing speeches, so I worked closely with Bernard Donoughue and mainly with Bernard on policy stuff.

Did he know Marcia before he arrived in No. 10?

I knew her by reputation in the '64–'70 period. The reputation was that she didn't get on with Derek Mitchell, that she got rid of him really and brought in Michael Halls, and Michael Halls was really her sort of 'creature' and then he wasn't and died.

I knew Derek Mitchell and he knew me, and my impression

was that there was quite some sort of jockeying between Derek and Marcia for Harold's attention.

Lord Butler was, of course, correct. Marcia was fighting for the creation of a brand-new political office which would deal with Harold's relationships with the Labour Party and the MPs, and the civil servants were fighting to continue to be the main men carrying out the Prime Minister and the government's policies. Lord Butler recalls:

I had some sense of what relationships were in No. 10 and my sense was that Derek and Marcia were not sort of natural chums. Derek Mitchell was quite a conventional civil servant.

As far as we in No. 10 were concerned, there was a natural loyalty to the Prime Minister, in this case Ted Heath. The Miners' Strike was a critical time with the three-day week and all that and I was the private secretary who was dealing with economic stuff and therefore principally the effects of the strike. I was working very long hours and writing speeches about who governs Britain and all that, so when Ted Heath went out it was a very traumatic moment for us. So when Harold came in I and the other private secretaries were not sure what was going to happen to us as it had all been pretty fraught.

But it turned out Harold knew how the system worked, he had been a civil servant himself and he didn't make any change to the civil service private secretary team in No. 10, and because the first thing on the agenda was the Miners' Strike, I worked very closely with him and I quickly discovered we had something in common. I had been an undergraduate at University College,

Oxford, where he had been a research fellow when he was working with Beveridge. We had a lot of acquaintances in common, so we always had something easy to talk about.

So I established an easy personal relationship with Harold and with Bernard because he was easy to establish a relationship with, and Joe Haines too. I hadn't known him before but that worked fine, so we were a group now. The political side – Marcia and Albert Murray and so on – they were always a bit separate. We were dealing with the policy and they were dealing with the politics, but from the beginning Marcia was a bloody nuisance and such a bloody nuisance that I could hardly believe it.

She would arrange commitments and engagements for Harold without any concern for what was in his official diary, clashing engagements and so on, using the Prime Minister's car when she wanted to go shopping or pick up her children from school and generally behaving in a way that for me, aged thirty-four and a slightly idealistic ingenuous civil servant, seemed to be completely shocking and of course all the more shocking because it was in contrast to the very austere days of Ted Heath, when everything was like a gentleman's club.

What I tried to do was keep out of her way, and she would interfere with briefings for parliamentary questions or statements that Harold was going to make, but on the whole if we could get away without her being involved we did our best to do that because, well, she was disruptive. She was more disruptive with the Prime Minister, with Harold, than she was with me.

Up until the arrival of Marcia, my career advanced because I was good at getting on with people and I had no strong political feelings at all. My job was to support the Prime Minister of the day and I thought it was a tremendous honour and privilege to be in No. 10. I thought how lucky I was to do that. I found it absolutely fascinating, as I think we all did, and therefore I was all the more shocked when Marcia was disrupting what I wanted to be a very smooth operation in support of the Prime Minister. I tried to keep out of her way, but when I had to spend time with her, this is where I come to what was pretty nearly my undoing. I chatted to her and tried to be as friendly as I could.

So, I tried to be on good terms with her.

As Robin Butler recalls, the incident with Marcia which nearly ruined his civil service career occurred after he had accompanied Harold Wilson to the 1974 Trades Union Congress as his speech-writer and general factotum.

He made his speech and I was sitting behind as a sort of bag carrier and making sure he had his notes and so on, but the consequence was that I was in the photos of him on the platform, with Sid Green and trade union leaders sitting beside and me just behind Harold.

Robin Butler thought he had got on well with the Prime Minister and the conference had been successful, but when he got back to Downing Street, Robert Armstrong called him into his office and said, 'I am afraid the Prime Minister wants you to return to the Treasury.'

Robin Butler was shocked. He was on a three-year secondment from the Treasury to No. 10, and he couldn't afford to be sacked by the Prime Minister.

I wanted to know what I had done wrong and Robert Armstrong said he didn't know what I had done wrong. He explained, 'The Prime Minister has just said he wants a change and he wants you to go back to the Treasury.' So I told Bernard Donoughue and Joe Haines, with whom by then I had formed quite a relationship through the summer, and they were shocked to hear that I was being thrown out and went and asked Harold what it was all about. Harold said, 'Marcia says he goes to *Private Eye* lunches.'

And it was true I had been to a *Private Eye* lunch. What happened was this: at University College, Richard Ingrams and I shared tutorials and so I had known Richard for ages and Paul Foot and all that. So I was friendly with them and they were doing a hatchet job on somebody called Nicholas Bethell. Nicholas Bethell had translated Solzhenitsyn's *Cancer Ward* and there were suggestions that he had got it through a man called Victor Louis, who was thought to be a 'fellow traveller' in London. Nicholas Bethell was then in the Lords. *Private Eye* thought he was a Soviet agent and ran this story, which led to Nicholas Bethell's resignation or at least to Ted Heath's sacking him from a government job. Ted Heath said, 'I don't want to take any risks with somebody, you know he is not important enough, as a Lords whip. I am not going to use any credit defending him.' So poor old Nicholas Bethell, who I am sure wasn't a Soviet agent at all, lost his job. So while Richard Ingrams and Paul Foot were running this, they did indeed invite me to a *Private Eye* lunch, and that must have been during Ted Heath's time and I went along to that lunch to defend Nicholas Bethell who was my friend, he had been a school friend and they had all sorts of wrong information about him at *Private Eye* which I put right. End of story.

But when the slagheap thing developed and *Private Eye* were going for Marcia and her family about that, I was travelling in the car with Marcia and being sympathetic with her and talking about how awful *Private Eye* were, and I told her the story about how they had got at my friend Nicholas Bethell and I had been to this lunch and they had all sorts of wrong information about him, and I had managed to put that right. I told her this story to be sympathetic with her about how ghastly *Private Eye* were, but I think she had stored this in her mind and when she decided that I was getting too close to Harold – I think it was the picture of me at the Trades Union Congress with Harold that did it – I think she decided that she wanted to get rid of me.

I had been telling her about that story where they got all the facts wrong and how I corrected it and she used it as a reason to get shot of me. I had never been to a *Private Eye* lunch either before or after that, I had just been to this one over Nicholas Bethell, but when she wanted to think of something to get rid of me, maybe because she got the impression that I was closer to Richard Ingrams than was comfortable, that was the excuse she used.

The press was much less intrusive in those days. *Private Eye* was out on a limb in terms of political scandal.

So my theory is that Marcia felt I was getting too close to Harold, and she did get rid of other people where she had felt that had happened. Thinking back on it, she might have thought I was a danger to her and Harold, but I doubt it. I think she decided Harold and I were getting on too well.

So Bernard and Joe asked me and I told them the story, and they went back to Harold and told him the truth and I got a reprieve.

So I served out my time and went back to the Treasury at the end of '75 having done my three-year secondment, so not having been returned in disgrace from there, my career flourished, but had I gone back to the Treasury in disgrace that would have been a big black mark.

I am very fond of Joe Haines, he was part of saving my career. I used to write boring correct speeches for Harold, and they were transformed by Joe into brilliant speeches. I shall always be grateful to him for that. Joe is a class warrior and a fighter.

By the time the situation between Robin Butler and Marcia surfaced, her behaviour had become very difficult indeed. There were still plenty of mentions in Bernard Donoughue's diaries of Marcia taking 'handfuls' of pills. Sometimes she was ill and then given more pills (there's no record of what they were) by Dr Joe Stone.

Around this time, there are also countless tales of hysterical outbursts and eccentric behaviour witnessed by staff and many visitors to No. 10.

On the evening of 15 May 1975, Bernard wrote:

There was a dinner for the Prime Minister of Fiji. We were all upstairs having drinks until 8.50, waiting for Marcia who arrived with Gerald Kaufman twenty minutes late ... The PM made a charming speech of welcome. Just as the Fijian Prime Minister was rising to reply, Marcia got up and stamped out of the room. She is heavy on her feet, so everybody noticed. Joe and I discussed it but had no idea what it was all about. After the meal the mystery was cleared up. Marcia returned to the reception room with her friend, the property developer Eric Miller, and the singer Frank

Sinatra. She was fawning all over Sinatra ... She took the PM off to speak to Sinatra. Joe blew up. All his puritanism came out. We gathered she wanted to attend the forthcoming Sinatra concert ... We left at midnight, by when the PM was looking very tired.

The rumour mill was working overtime in the mid-1970s, as tales of Marcia's outbursts abounded. Harold Wilson's official driver Bill Housden often reported the latest hot gossip to Bernard.

On 20 February 1976, Bernard wrote:

Bill Housden told me Marcia and H. W. had a twenty-minute row in the car outside Lord North Street, with her still attacking him because he was retiring. As he got out of the car, he said, 'After what you have said, I am even more determined than ever to go.'

17

Harold Wilson's Resignation

On 5 April 1976, I had been working at *World in Action* at Granada Television for two years. Harold Wilson had been Prime Minister for just a few weeks longer. In 1972, I had been on attachment to the BBC in Northern Ireland directing local programmes. I had taken part enthusiastically in the first 1974 election in the Mid Ulster constituency, trying hard to get my head around the proportional voting system they had there even back then, and hoping very hard that a man called John Dunlop wouldn't defeat Bernadette Devlin McAliskey, but he did.

I went back to Manchester and decided it was time for me to move on from the BBC. I wrote to Gus Macdonald, who was the then boss at *World in Action*, and asked for a job. I got one with amazing speed. It didn't take me long to find out why. There were endless rows going on at Granada because nearly all the glamour boys who worked on *WIA* wanted to live and work from London. The people who ran Granada, Lord Bernstein and David Plowright, were always incredibly strong about their rock-solid relationship with the north-west, so much so that eventually it became known as Granadaland. Gus Macdonald couldn't believe his luck when someone turned up asking for a job as a director working and living in Manchester or thereabouts. It would be a sock in the eye for the London-based glamour boys. I must have spun a plausible tale of my skills and talents, and began working ferociously hard, always on stories, in the UK, the minute I arrived. All the boys wanted to get abroad fast to war zones or the USA and hated having to go local. My first ever *WIA* was a tale of pyramid selling in the Midlands.

On 5 April, I got the train to London, dashed out and caught a taxi from King's Cross to the House of Commons. I can't remember for the life of me why, but I was going to lunch with Joe Ashton, the Labour MP for Bassetlaw. As the taxi rumbled through central London, I began to see newspaper billboards screaming 'Prime Minister Resigns' and 'Harold Quits'. I still remember the thrill of something really big happening, and me feeling part of it.

Just over a year before, I had made a profile of Margaret Thatcher for *World in Action* entitled 'Why I Want to Be Leader by Margaret Thatcher'. It had been my idea – I fought hard for it, as no one else thought she had a chance of winning or wanted to film in a graveyard in Finchley on a Saturday night dance in the constituency. It was broadcast on 4 February and seven days later, her wish and mine came true and she became the first woman to lead a UK political party.

The boys were suitably horrified. Clive James, TV reviewer for *The Observer*, wrote how *World in Action* lefties must have loathed it, but I had had the same excited feeling of being part of a major event.

I thought Joe Ashton might stand me up for the lunch date, but he didn't. We went to the Members' Dining Room which was crowded with chattering MPs and their guests. I can't remember a word of what we or anyone else said, as once again I was gripped by the excitement of being involved in something important, happening now. By the time lunch was over, there was a message from the boss to say that we were going to make a programme about the runners and riders and the betting odds in the Labour leadership. We set up a gossip station in an upstairs room at the St Stephen's Tavern across the road. The campaign managers were encouraged to drop in at any time and report on their candidate's progress.

While all this was going on, Marcia and Harold were wrapping things up at No. 10 and preparing for their futures outside politics. We all know how it was for Harold. The newspapers were full of suggestions why he had given up. All his political life, he had believed he could go when he pleased. It had been a strengthener for him, like in lots of marriages. Who hasn't felt cheered by telling themselves 'I don't have to put up with this'?

Barbara Castle wasn't so sure. 'Has one the right to throw our party into turmoil for no apparent cause? To face them with a fait accompli because one knows they would plead with one to stay if they knew in time?'

Loads of journalists and politicians were still looking for an answer to the eternal question 'What is Harold up to?' Was he sidestepping a gathering crisis? Was it one of the clouds of scandal which had passed over Parliament in the past few years? The Marcia land deals affair? The Jeremy Thorpe scandal? The fringe banking crash in London? And, of course, many were sure that Marcia was the real reason – perhaps, worse than sex, it was Marcia plus sex and money?

Lord Donoughue told me that Harold Wilson had told him plainly many months before the actual event that he'd done a deal with Mary. He would give the office up when he was sixty and they could have a new life in Oxford or Cambridge. He knew that was the way to please her. Her displeasure with his long prime ministership was never covered up or disguised, just like the constant pressure on Tony Blair to stand out of the way of Gordon Brown. Harold hoped to become head of a college; Mary would love being an Oxford wife again. But it didn't happen like that. Harold had got a reputation for being tricky and he was passed over by both his first choice, University College in Oxford where he had worked with Sir William Beveridge, and Trinity College in Cambridge. To add insult to injury, it was his close friend and lawyer Lord Goodman, who had done so much to help Harold in the war with the press, who became master of University College.

To make things worse for Mary, the Wilsons needed somewhere to live and ended up buying a flat in Ashley Gardens, where we too had a London flat. Just a short walk from the House of Commons, the 1890s mansion blocks are well seasoned with MPs of just about every party and their families, along with distinguished civil servants and retired leaders of the armed forces and captains of industry, male and female.

Marcia had made vigorous attempts to stop Harold resigning, but she failed. She seemed to understand so much better than everyone else what it would be like to relinquish power. It was all very well to resign from being Prime Minister, but it was even tougher for Marcia to lose her job as his sidekick. Her boys were eight and seven and their existence had been revealed to the world only a couple of years before. She was forty-four and single and at the very least she needed to support them for another ten years.

The children were now part of Baroness Falkender's public life, and she alone was responsible for supporting them, bringing them up and educating them. Like all mums, she wanted the best for them. Extraordinarily, in 1979 the *Telegraph Sunday Magazine* tried to help. A journalist called Denis Hart was brought over from Ireland to interview Marcia. Presumably, English journalists who had followed and stalked Marcia and spent days waiting on her front doorstep could not be trusted to do the kind of soft-focus portrait that might keep Marcia happy.

Denis Hart spent several days with Marcia and her sons in her country house just a couple of miles from Harold Wilson's farm house in Great Missenden, and her London home in Wyndham Mews.

Hart began by writing that he had caught Marcia up with what the newspapers had been saying about her lately. He doesn't tell us what they had said but gives us her reaction to his quote: 'Oh, that won't do, it really will not do. That is deeply offensive.'

Most of the interview is trivial stuff, a plea for some sympathy for Marcia. But there is a set of extraordinary and beautiful photos by Tim Mercer of Marcia and her boys, Marcia with Harold and Mary at home and Marcia with her sister and brother. I spoke to Tim Mercer, who is still taking great photos today. He hadn't accompanied the journalist, he didn't know the story and he had met Marcia and her boys alone. He thought they were a cheerful and lovely family and said he had spent some time playing football with the boys in the garden before Marcia had taken him off to meet Harold and Mary.

In Denis Hart's interview, we learn that Marcia is usually dressed from head to toe by Marks and Spencer and that she has a bowl of Heinz low-calorie soup and a piece of wholemeal bread for her lunch if she is at home in London. Harold's driver Bill Housden picks her up every morning and drives her to the Commons, or shopping or to an engagement. Intriguingly, today it is lunch with Lady Annabel Goldsmith at Luigi's in the King's Road. She then spends the afternoon at the Institute of Directors listening to Sir James Goldsmith, General Haig and Sir Bernard Miles. The article continues to describe social engagements with the titled, the rich and the famous with regular comings and goings chauffeured by Bill Housden in the government car supplied to Harold Wilson. Long phone chats with Harold and regular visits to his homes are also recorded.

The journalist mentions Harold Wilson's resignation honours list on 'purple paper' and Marcia responds with, 'Lavender, please. The description is immensely important. I have become attached to it.' She continues:

I was walking between the stairs and the study in No. 10 follow-ing behind Harold, and I think it was the only paper available on which to jot down the names he gave me as we went along. To this day, I do not know why there was any coloured paper around. It certainly was not mine. It was all done very quickly.

Then they talk briefly about the awesome responsibility of having certain matters delegated to you by the Prime Minister, and sudden-ly Marcia seems to speak from the heart: 'I used to wish that Harold would burst into the room and say, "Don't worry, I will handle that," but he never did.' Confirming once again my belief that Harold and Marcia were a partnership, very much like a successful marriage where both partners rely on the support of the other.

Marcia obviously feels throughout the interview that she needs to make it clear that she is not a rich woman and that it is going to be a great struggle bringing up the boys the way she wants on very little money. 'I have about £2,500 in the Abbey National Building Society. I have no investments, no private income.'

The journalist then changes the topic, putting forward a reasonable question: hadn't No. 10 introduced her to interesting people who had now become her friends? Marcia disagreed – given the long, unforgiving hours she had to work in Downing Street, there was little time to go out and meet people, even at weekends. 'Your life is not your own. I suppose there were times when I should have said, "Oh, to hell with that. I have got my own life to lead." But I really did believe that I had to be on duty.'

The article ends with a quote from Lord Weidenfeld, who played a very important part in the lives of Harold and Marcia and published books by both of them. The journalist asks him why he thought Marcia had had such a consistently hostile press.

'Because she was young, attractive and a woman,' he replied.

18

The Lavender List

For over a century, the British honours system has been a hot topic. Controversy arises every time a new list of awards is published. We seem convinced that many of the people honoured couldn't possibly have deserved their recognition or done the work described. We've come up with new explanations for abbreviations such as OBE: 'other buggers' efforts'. But however much we sneer, it seems most of us across the Commonwealth would be delighted to accept an honour, the grander the better.

In New Zealand in the 1990s and early 2000s, Labour Prime Minister Helen Clark and her government got rid of the British titles of 'knight' and 'dame' at the top of the New Zealand honours pyramid and replaced them with local grades of the New Zealand Order of Merit (ONZ).

When Labour lost the NZ general election in 2008, an early move of the incoming National government was to revert immediately to the former system and announce a conversion scheme. Those who had been made Principal and Distinguished Companions of the Order of Merit were able to apply to have the letters after their names changed back to the old titles. This they did with tremendous enthusiasm. Once again knights and dames sprang up across the land and are still being appointed. The actor Sam Neill has suddenly become 'Sir Sam' decades after his honour was gazetted.

Back in 1922 in the UK, David Lloyd George didn't exactly hand out a price list but those in the know were aware that a knighthood went for around £10,000 and a peerage five times that. In the 1922 birthday honours, Joseph Robinson, a gold and diamond magnate convicted of fraud, became Sir Joseph; and William Vestey, a meat importer notorious for tax evasion, was dubbed Sir William. Three years later, the Honours (Prevention of Abuses) Act became law and the sale of peerages and any other honours became illegal.

Half a century later, there was much gossip and huge scandal surrounding Harold Wilson's resignation honours list. Roy Jenkins said Wilson's retirement was disfigured by his eccentric list. But why blame the Prime Minister when there was a woman by his side who could take the rap?

Immortalised as the 'Lavender List', the 1976 suggestions, written by Marcia herself in blue ink with corrections by Harold in red, were believed by many to have been solely Marcia's attempt to reward her own friends and supporters.

No one was accusing Prime Minister Harold Wilson of selling honours; the implication was that Marcia had so much power over him that she could hand out awards to whoever she fancied or perhaps fancied her. Many Westminster and Whitehall trusties, including head of the press office Joe Haines, were by now thoroughly fed up with Marcia's intemperate behaviour, so the accusation landed at the door of Baroness Falkender.

Joe Haines described the list as 'lavender' because it was written on coloured paper in Marcia's own hand. His wife Irene protested mildly that he was colour blind for the paper was more pink than purple, but she was ignored and the 'Lavender List' caught on immediately and made great newspaper headlines.

Marcia said she didn't know where the coloured paper had come from, it was just what she happened to have in her hand when the Prime Minister had asked her to make a note. She insisted the list represented Harold's wishes. All she had done was jotted down a few of his suggestions as he spoke to her walking in the corridor, and the paper wasn't hers personally – she'd never seen it before – it was just something she grabbed at the time.

The idea that Harold and Marcia might have collaborated on the list was beyond Joe Haines's belief in the structure of the Downing Street hierarchy. Harold was Prime Minister; Marcia was a secretary, and she had no right to present her own views. But Marcia had spent the whole of her political life presenting her views to Harold, supporting him and promoting him as 'the leader'. The thing that seemed to anger Joe and his colleagues the most was the idea that Marcia was bossing Harold about, telling him what to do.

We can understand today, given the long and successful relationship of Harold and Marcia, that she may well have told him forcefully who she thought should be honoured. But he would have contributed at least equally to the discussion and, as always, they would have come to an amiable compromise.

The Wilson papers in the Bodleian Library contain file after file of carbon copies of letters written on behalf of the Prime Minister by Marcia, frequently with neatly handwritten notes. 'Is this OK with you? Marcia' with 'Fine by me, H. W.' in response. Everything was a collaborative discussion between the pair.

The great storm created by Wilson's resignation honours list would be unlikely to happen today. Bernard Delfont, Lew Grade and Max Rayne – who if not household names would certainly be familiar to older readers – were all made peers in 1976 for their services to theatre, television or the arts. Also on the list were George Weidenfeld, the chairman of one of the largest British publishing firms, and John Vaizey, professor of economics at Brunel University. And, of course, Joe Stone, Harold Wilson's close friend and personal physician, became Lord Stone. These were just the sort of names that have been appearing in honours lists from Prime Ministers from both sides of the House before Harold Wilson's governments and ever since.

However, the names which caused the controversy were James Goldsmith, Eric Miller and Joseph Kagan and one name which had been rejected outright: David Frost. Frost had been the negotiator of the deal between Harold and Yorkshire Television for the series *A Prime Minister on Prime Ministers* which Harold signed up for as soon as he ceased being Prime Minister.

James Goldsmith was the one name on the list which was hard to explain and may well have been Marcia's contribution. Richard Ingrams, who was the first editor of *Private Eye*, suggested an intriguing possibility in an *Independent* article on Francis Wheen's BBC docudrama *The Lavender List*:

Perhaps I am biased on this score because it is undoubtedly true that, in 1976, Marcia encouraged Sir James Goldsmith, with whom she enjoyed a close relationship, to destroy *Private Eye*, of which I was then editor.

She did so partly to revenge herself on the *Eye*, which, in 1974, had exposed the extent of her influence over Wilson as well as revealing the existence of her two children by the *Daily Mail's* political editor, Walter Terry ... Goldsmith not only issued 64 writs on his own behalf but set up a fund to enable others to sue.

Luckily for us, the plot misfired. As a result, partly, of the publicity generated by all the writs, Goldsmith was deprived of the peerage which Falkender had put down for him on her famous Lavender List. He had to be content with a knighthood.

Like many aspects of the Falkender story, Goldsmith's citation 'for services to exports and ecology' has never been fully explained. But the campaign against the *Eye* showed the dangers of getting involved in litigation.

The other two names at the heart of the dispute were Eric Miller and Joseph Kagan, who were part of the Kitchen Cabinet and had both made substantial donations towards running Wilson's office. Joe Kagan didn't just favour Harold Wilson. He made generous donations to the Labour Party, both regionally in Yorkshire and nationally. He was, right from the beginning of his friendship with Harold Wilson, the strongest supporter of the Prime Minister and also of Marcia.

It was after they had been ennobled that both Miller and Kagan had trouble with the law, from within the companies they had originally built and handed over to others.

Miller built the Peachey Property Corporation – the biggest residential property company in Britain. But there were inquiries by the Department of Trade and the City of London police fraud squad into possible misallocation of company assets and he resigned as chairman and stockholders voted to dismiss him. One of the charges against Sir Eric was that he ordered a million-pound plane for Peachey without authorisation from his board of directors. The company also had suits against him for hundreds of thousands of pounds, including two charging that he had improperly obtained a necklace and a racehorse with company funds. Sir Eric didn't wait for the court case. He shot himself in the head and died of his wounds. He had lent Harold Wilson his private helicopter during the 1974 election campaign.

To those of us who knew Joe Kagan and the support he had given locally in West Yorkshire to the people who worked for his company, to local good causes and to the Elland Labour Party, his prosecution for stealing bolts of indigo cloth from Kagan Textiles, the 'crimes' for which he was sent to prison, were dubious. There were sympathetic chuckles in the pubs and Pennine hill villages like mine and thinly veiled opinions that 'those Tory buggers' had got Joe in the end. In his obituary of Lord Kagan in *The Independent*, Tam Dalyell, MP for Linlithgow for forty-three years, wrote:

> The relationship between Wilson and Kagan, who was knighted in 1970 and created a life peer in Wilson's 1976 resignation hon-ours list, was the cause of much comment, never more so than when, in December 1979, warrants were issued for his arrest. The warrants alleged conspiracy to defraud the public revenue and to falsify records ...
>
> The real trouble was perhaps not Kagan's financial affairs but what was perceived to be his continuing East European connec-tions, which aroused the interest of the secret service.

It was discovered that Kagan was friends with Richardas Vai-gauskas, a fellow Lithuanian who was known to be a KGB officer. Their relationship flourished because both men were passionately keen on chess and Kagan certainly wanted to keep on the good side of influential Lithuanian Russians in order to assist his own relatives back in Vilnius. However, evidence of the friendship caused an enormous hoo-ha at the time because of its potential to embarrass Harold Wilson.

In the end, Kagan was fined £375,000 and served a ten-month sentence in Rudgate Open Prison, North Yorkshire. Here he taught many of his fellow inmates to play chess, and he was admired for his skill and dexterity at sewing. Dalyell suggested that where many members of the House of Lords would simply have crumbled in prison, Joe Kagan found it a picnic compared to German concentration camps and the Russian Army he had dealt with in his youth.

Kagan was evidently very hurt that the knighthood which Harold Wilson had given him was withdrawn, but this made him all the more determined to reappear in the House of Lords. As an ex-prisoner, he made uniquely valuable contributions to debates on penal matters and wrote powerful letters to the press.

Tam Dalyell, who was a true parliamentarian of the old school, followed what went on at Westminster carefully. He went to watch Kagan make his maiden speech in the House of Lords:

> It was very powerful. He believed that we lived in the midst of a desperate contest for the soul of man. It was between democracy and dictatorship ... One knew that this was a man who spoke not from theory or reading but experience of five years of Stalin and Hitler ...
>
> By coming back to the House of Lords after his term of imprisonment Joseph Kagan displayed considerable guts. In my opinion Kagan was a man whose contribution to Britain far and away outweighed any of the naughty things which he may have done.

From the day Harold and Marcia met in the 1950s, Joseph Kagan was a generous and understanding friend to both of them. Harold needed his help with funds to run his office, particularly in opposition where no government funds were provided, and Joe was incredibly helpful when Marcia was about to give birth and he dispatched the Kagans' nanny Pauline to care for her and the baby. Over their lifetimes, Joe helped Marcia with finance for several properties, including the flat over St James's Park Tube station where Tim was taken to be cared for by Pauline for the first couple of weeks of his life. Joseph Kagan proved to be discreet as well as generous in his support. I knew Joe Kagan and his family and I liked them all. There was no doubt that Joe was warm-hearted, enthusiastic and generous with everyone he came in touch with. It was as if he could never quite believe that he had come through the terrible years in the ghetto and the concentration camps and landed with golden good fortune in the hills that surrounded the Calder Valley. He was joyous and pleased to see every person he met and wanted to share his great good fortune with them all.

Today there are strict and complicated rules about how much and from where benefactors can give financial support to political parties. Both Labour and the Conservatives have been investigated about cash for peerages and no political party has been prosecuted under the 1925 Act. There was never any suggestion that Harold Wilson was less than scrupulously honest in financial dealings, but many people were eager to blame Marcia for anything questionable. As head of the press office, Joe Haines's job was to present his Prime Minister in the best possible light. But as time went on and he became more and more outraged by Marcia's behaviour, he began to think that Marcia was the Queen of the Dodgy Deal and it was her hold over an increasingly weak and foolish Harold which caused everything to go wrong.

There is no evidence at all that Lady Falkender wrote her own list of those deserving peerages and slapped it down in front of Harold saying, 'Implement this!' The squalls and thunderstorms over the resignation honours happened in 1976, in the not-so-far-off days before mobile phones and computers in every office. People had typewriters and secretaries, and secretaries had pens and scrap paper, could do shorthand and often wrote things down while their boss peered over their shoulder. What could have been more normal than Harold Wilson and his political secretary discussing his resignation honours list together? There is no doubt that they would have done that. That was how they dealt with most matters: they discussed them and, if they agreed, implemented them.

If the 'Lavender List' had been from the office of Theresa May or Boris Johnson, it would have been accepted as a bog standard presentation of awards to those who had helped the political parties to survive with generous donations. From this distance and knowing what we now know about Marcia, whose mental health had been in steady decline since the birth of her sons and who was taking amphetamines in the morning and Valium at night to get her through the long and difficult days, it is certainly possible that she added a few suggestions to the list to discuss with Harold. 'Suggestions and discussions' had been very much part of the way they worked together since Marcia started out with Harold in 1956. But to say that the entire Lavender List was masterminded by Marcia would be short-sighted and inaccurate.

After Harold's resignation as Prime Minister, he stayed on as a backbencher in the House of Commons for seven years and Marcia continued to run his life. Bill Housden, his driver through all his time as Prime Minister, continued to drive him and Marcia. Both Harold and Marcia continued to make money where they could. Harold did a big series, *A Prime Minister on Prime Ministers*, arranged by his friend David Frost with Yorkshire Television. It was not a great success. Harold seemed to have lost his rugged gutsy style that had seen him have great successes in the chamber of the House of Commons, and he didn't seem so comfortable on television any more.

Marcia began a contract with the *Daily Mail* for a weekly column, 'The other side of politics', which seemed to last for years. Sometimes she had a go at politicians she knew disliked her:

> Roy Hattersley is telling people that if I ever refer to him again as an old friend in this column he will sue ... Before Roy manages to rewrite the history books completely, perhaps I should confess just to embarrass him still further that I was one of the few people during the Wilson years to risk considerable unpopularity, not least with my colleagues, for speaking up for Roy.

Occasionally she criticised Margaret Thatcher, but she never scored a direct hit:

> It's only six months since the last eve of session dinner party for ministers at 10 Downing Street ... The tradition was a modest reception for members of the government at which the Queen's Speech was read aloud. The PM gave a pep-talk after which everyone went their separate ways for dinner with their wives.

Dull stuff. You couldn't imagine that *Mail on Sunday* readers got much of a thrill out of such matters.

But Marcia always managed to highlight in her articles the lack of women in every career category at Westminster:

> If anyone still believes that the combination of militant feminism and a woman Prime Minister has done anything for the general lot of women, I have news for them.
>
> There are now 23 women MPs, one more than in the last parliament, one less than the 24 elected in 1945.
>
> The Labour Party has the most to be ashamed of. In 1945 there were 21 women Labour MPs.
>
> Today there are only ten.

Joe Haines says that Marcia became so disappointed with the Labour Party that before the 1979 election, she wrote to Margaret Thatcher and offered to help her win it. Joe, who is as tribal as Alastair Campbell, was horrified, but I could see how Marcia must have felt. It was so exciting back then to see a woman on the cusp of power that many women felt the same way. In 1997, when I was interviewing the new female members of Parliament, Ruth Kelly, who was one of Labour's brightest stars, told me that it was Margaret Thatcher's success which had inspired her interest in politics all those years before as a Westminster schoolgirl.

Marcia Falkender could have been an inspiration too, but she was doing the wrong job at the wrong time. Her role as right-hand woman to the Prime Minister, the person with the organisational skills who took the intellectual ability and political beliefs of Harold Wilson and presented them to the voters in an acceptable form that they wanted to vote for, was not a front-facing job. It was crucial but without a public profile.

19

The After Party

When Harold Wilson and Marcia Falkender left Downing Street, it wasn't as if they were in their twilight years. Harold was sixty and Marcia just forty-four when he resigned the leadership. For a long time after, there was intense speculation as to why he left so suddenly and so young. I believe he had done a deal with Mary, who hated the rough and tumble and the innuendo of Westminster, and had put a reasonable time limit on how long they should stay in politics. Bernard Donoughue told me he had heard the same story from Harold himself just weeks before he made his announcement. Of course, Marcia had tried very hard to stop him going. For her, it would be the end of everything she held so dear and enjoyed so much, but I believe he was absolutely determined. They both had incomes to earn and separate lives to live, but Marcia couldn't really picture that. Harold stayed on as a backbench MP until 1983, writing his biography, making television programmes and hoping but failing to become master of an Oxford college to reward Mary at last with the quiet academic family life she had so longed for. Marcia continued to work for Harold but in a much reduced role. Answering a few letters from constituents and typing up the boss's memoirs were no replacement for what she had managed in Downing Street, and the lifestyle she had enjoyed as the Prime Minister's right-hand woman.

Marcia was facing a difficult future bringing up her two sons in a society which still had a long way to go before illegitimate offspring were treated equally. When asked about them, she now spoke carefully about Tim and Dan in public without ever referring to their father by name.

The exclusivity of Downing Street, her years inside No. 10 and her incredible doorstep bust-ups with legions of press photographers and journalists had certainly not prepared Marcia to begin a life in a modest terraced house in the London suburbs with her kids at the local state school. Nor did she want a return to rural Northamptonshire to join her brother Tony and his wife in Blisworth. Although she still espoused socialism and when she spoke publicly at all spoke loudly and clearly in its defence, she also seemed to be stating she was Baroness Falkender now, and she wanted to live like a baroness. For the rest of her life, she yearned for privacy and seclusion. She wanted taxis and hire cars, private education for her children and security for all her family. She was looking for protection from the horrors she had suffered in the decade which began with the birth of her children and ended with her unsuccessful and emotional pleas to Harold to stay on as Prime Minister. Now she needed to earn a sizeable income, but what were the chances of that? She continued to work as Harold's secretary and for a few years she wrote a gossipy yet rather dull politics column for the *Mail on Sunday* – it had few scoops and garnered little attention. Marcia, as she admitted when asked by the journalist friends of Harold charged with improving her image, did not want to be a public person. Her joy had come from being at the heart of the British government, administering a

Labour Prime Minister she loved and had done much to create and seeing the results of their joint endeavours improving life in Britain. The column limped along and was eventually cancelled. There were no offers from the Labour Party by leaders Jim Callaghan, Michael Foot or Neil Kinnock to use Marcia's enormous skills to benefit the party, which has had to wait a very long time for these skills to return – until Keir Starmer had the perspicacity to hire Sue Gray.

What else could Marcia do to find the money to bring up her boys? She believed her only other option was to refer back to her period in No. 10 with Harold and to ask for help from people she believed she had helped in their careers, and as she became older that became an embarrassingly expanded group in the Lords. Many were in denial that she'd ever helped anyone. Others referred back to Harold Wilson's resignation honours and suggested she had sold them to anyone who might help her out. But some did give her a helping hand and paid for her treatment in private hospitals as she got older and less well.

It was wrong, immoral and heartbreaking that Marcia Williams, who had made such an important contribution to the 1960s and '70s Labour governments and who after the birth of her sons became heavily drug dependent and increasingly disinhibited, should start begging for help from those she believed she had previously helped.

Marcia had been positively encouraged by Harold Wilson's medical adviser Joe Stone to keep increasing her daily dose of benzodiazepines, which he believed, in line with legions of other doctors in the 1960s and '70s, would control her hysteria, panic and anxiety. He feared that without these drugs she might destroy the Prime Minister. We know now, of course, that the effect of the drugs was probably the reverse, and that addiction was hard to break. 'Tougher than heroin,' said Professor Malcolm Lader of the Institute of Psychiatry. In 1978, he called benzodiazepines 'the opium of the masses':

Benzodiazepine tranquillisers can make people much more suggestible and vulnerable to be being taken advantage of while taking the drug. There are cases in which people have shoplifted, crashed cars and behaved violently while under the influence of benzodiazepines which are comparable to the effects of alcohol. Valium is a long-acting drug which has a cumulative effect and so while there may be fluctuations in the level of confusion, there would be no lucid moments ... A person's judgement, insight, memory, ability to plan and perceptions are all impaired.

Whether Marcia continued to take benzodiazepines and purple hearts after leaving Downing Street is unknown, but she would likely have continued to face many negative effects from her long-term use and possible addiction.

Harold was worried about Marcia. He believed she had been unfairly treated by many of her colleagues, he knew she had to educate her boys and support her unemployed mother and sister, so he talked to his friends and asked them to give her a helping hand. For years Marcia had desperately avoided all contact with the press and the media, but now everyone knew the story of her life and loves and her two boys. Harold asked his friends in television if there was a way they could give Marcia some publicity which might help with her new life and career. So Thames Television, the London weekday programme provider, agreed to help and scheduled a cosy and warm thirty-minute interview with their superstar presenter Judith Chalmers. She had been a top woman at the BBC presenting

Woman's Hour and *Come Dancing* before it became *Strictly*. Now she was the key figure in a hugely popular holiday show *Wish You Were Here...?*

Judith and I were working at Thames at the same time, so when I started writing this book I rang her to ask what she had thought of Marcia, but fifty years later her dominant memory was her own nervousness at having to do a political interview. At Thames in those days, you had to be male and called Jonathan Dimbleby, Alastair Burnet or Llew Gardner to qualify to ask questions of politicians. Judith gave Marcia a comfortable ride and the programme was cheerful and watchable. It's certainly a unique piece of television history as the only television interview Marcia ever gave.

Judith had a carefully prepared introduction:

For eight and a half years, Marcia Falkender was at the right hand of the most powerful man in Britain, the Prime Minister Harold Wilson.

In that time she had an extraordinary view of the way power is exercised in this country to the point where her critics believed her to be a political power herself.

From her childhood in Northamptonshire, where her education started in the local primary school, she rose through university to work in Labour Party headquarters at Transport House before becoming Harold Wilson's political and personal secretary. She was a spectator as the strings of power were pulled, although she never pulled them herself. Or did she?

A member of the Labour government once said, 'Any man who gets on the wrong side of Marcia Williams is a fool.' So, in fact, did government ministers have reason to be in awe of you?

Marcia replied carefully: 'Yes, I suppose so, but then they would have been equally in awe of any man near the Prime Minister too. I think this has been overdrawn and exaggerated simply because I was a woman. It has lent an additional dimension to it, but an unreal one really.'

Judith then explained what was expected of a political secretary, and Marcia claimed full credit for inventing the job:

> Yes, I started that role. We came into office in '64 after thirteen years of a Conservative government and I had been running Harold Wilson's political office for a very long time – eight years before he became leader of the party and then two more years till he became Prime Minister, so I had had a very long stretch. But the civil service didn't see a role for a political secretary in Downing Street. He on the other hand had come to rely on my judgement and to rely on the sort of role I had played in relation to the party both in the country and in Parliament, so he wanted me there. So when we went into No. 10, I went in and a role for a political secretary was then created with a political office, which I think is essential.
>
> Most people forget that the Prime Minister is not just that – he is also the head of his party and he needs not just civil service advice on how to run the government; he needs advice about how to run his party and what's going on inside it. The whole sort of liaison between him and his party – or her and her party, should we ever get a Labour woman Prime Minister – well, obviously, in my view, is a very essential role.

Judith then asked nervously just how powerful Marcia was in No. 10.

Marcia considered:

I didn't think it was that powerful a role at the time. When you are living through events, at the time you don't always understand totally the dimension of it all. You just get on with your job, and my job was to organise him politically so that the party knew what he was doing and he knew what the party was doing. I acted as his ears and eyes and I organised things within Downing Street which were essentially political things and I just went about my business and I didn't realise it had become a sort of very important job. It was only later on, and frankly after I had left, that I realised the sort of importance that others had attached to it.

When I spoke to Joe Haines about Marcia the politician, he was derisory about her skills, saying she would never have succeeded in the House of Commons because she couldn't make public speeches. Perhaps he was wrong there. The interview with Judith Chalmers seems honest and accurate.

Marcia was concise and truthful about the job she had done, and broadened it out by tying what she and Harold were doing in Downing Street to the progress the Democrats were trying to make in the USA.

Marcia said that they believed it had been time for a change equivalent to what was happening in the USA. Jack Kennedy had become President and got America moving again. That was just what she and Harold were successful in doing in the UK.

'And therefore for us it was very exciting and we were on a sort of high. We went in there thinking this has been wonderful', reminisced Marcia.

Judith asked about Jack Kennedy. Was his success because he was such a dynamic and powerful man? Is that how Marcia felt about Harold Wilson? Did she feel that she was promoting a party or a particular man?

Marcia gave a real politician's answer:

Well, primarily it was the party of course, because it was a party of change, but also it was the man, because the man himself was typical of what had happened. He had come from a very ordinary background, lower middle class, working class really. He had won scholarships to school and a brilliant scholarship to Oxford.

Harold Wilson sort of expressed for all of us what had happened in Britain – the sort of rise of ordinary people and opportunity for everyone to get to the top – and I think that's how people saw him, thinking this could happen to my son. Here is this little boy photographed on the steps of 10 Downing Street – and we have all seen that picture of him in his big cap standing there at the age of ten – and everyone thought this could happen to my boy too.

Judith wondered if Marcia had foreseen a political future for herself when she was at school?

Yes, I loved history and I was quite good at it, but I was very fortunate in having a French teacher, Janet Margesson, who was in fact the daughter of the Tory Chief Whip at the time but she was very left wing and absolutely devoted to changing everything socially and politically. And she was also a terrific teacher, interested in girls and she used to take us on one side and not just talk to us about French and the wonderful things that were going on in France but she also talked to us about the things which were going on in Britain. I learned a lot from her about Labour and socialist politics.

I haven't really moved from where I was then. I think others have moved. I think that I probably typify all those people who would see the old Labour Party as owing more to Methodism than to Marxism. I think mine is a very Christian-based socialism because I want to see more fairness and justice. I don't like to see people not getting a fair crack of the whip.

Then Marcia expressed a great keenness for nationalisation:

I think some of the big industries could have been nationalised – they needed to be made more accountable. Many industries lend themselves to be owned by the state. In fact they are in European countries – France, Germany, Scandinavia: I think it has become a thing for them to either own the industries completely or to have a very major stake in it. I think that there are certainly things like the railways and coal which we now have an argument about. We forget that the coal industry was bankrupt after the war, really shed bitter tears about being taken over.

Judith moved the interview on to the Field family, who were all at one time working with Marcia and Harold: 'And you have one sister, Peggy, and one brother, Tony. All have been involved with the Labour Party?'

'Only by default really,' said Marcia, rapidly coming up with an explanation very different from Joe Haines's accusation that by dragging all her family in with her, Marcia had more power over Harold:

> Simply because what people don't remember about the Harold Wilson years was that there was very little help in the way of state funding.
>
> Nowadays the state provides the Leader of the Opposition with vast sums of money and a car and he gets approximately £365,000 a year which he can then allocate around. A great part of it he keeps for his own private office. In my time, we got nothing at all. It had to be done by voluntary help or in other ways and my family were great volunteers. They believed in the whole thing; they thought it was a crusade, a new departure and they wanted to help out if they could, but they only became involved in a very indirect way really.

Judith allowed all this to pass without comment and asked Marcia what she felt like when Harold offered her a peerage.

It was a feature of Marcia's relationship with Harold Wilson that he was very good at listening to Marcia's minor grievances against her colleagues and ignoring them, but he really did believe that the Tories and the press had set Marcia up as a target. Hit on Marcia, get Harold. He was sure they were determined to ruin the Labour government's chances of winning the 1974 election by highlighting Tony Field's investments in waste and landfill in Ince-in-Makerfield near Wigan and focusing on the fact that all the other members of the Field family including Marcia owned shares in the company. But the courts had been clear that no wrongdoing had been committed

by any members of the Field family, so just a few weeks after Labour
had won the first 1974 election with a tiny majority, Harold defiantly
made Marcia a peer and Baroness Falkender was ennobled.

Judith asked boldly if Marcia had requested a peerage?

'No,' said Marcia firmly. 'I didn't want it because I don't particularly like the front end of politics. I loathe the theatrical end of politics.'

'Oh,' giggled Judith. 'I would have thought you loved the
limelight?'

Marcia sighed: 'No, I am a very private person really. I used to
loathe going to the House of Commons and listening to Harold
speak and I would have dodged it if I could. I used to sit and wince.
All that muttering and chuntering and shouting abuse at you.'

'But you did accept in the end,' countered Judith. 'What about
your visits to the House of Lords, then? What do you think you will
talk about in your maiden speech, because you have still not made
it, have you?'

Marcia said:

No, I haven't, but I know the moment I do I shall be hooked on
it. My own view of politics is that it is almost like a junkie and
drugs or alcohol – you get hooked on it. They all get hooked on
it. The best thing I could have done when I left No. 10 was to
form 'Politics Anonymous' and sit on the end of the phone and
any time anyone wanted to get back into the House I would say,
'Hang on, I will come over and have a quick word with you and
dissuade you.'

They both laughed at the obvious truth of this and then Judith
changed direction completely: 'There is a lot of fascination about

the power of a politician. I think that women find men in power sexually very attractive. There is a pull towards them.'

Marcia responded immediately and firmly:

Yes, well, I don't find them very attractive. I find men in politics completely unattractive, and I find men outside politics extremely attractive. I find that the world outside politics is much more interesting from that point of view.

In politics, I think they are very blinkered and single minded. They are sublimated creatures. One of my waspish friends (not in the Cabinet) said they are all sexual cripples, and in a way that describes them accurately in that their emotions have had to be channelled. They have had to sublimate a very great part of their private lives in order to operate in the very unreal atmosphere.

Some girls I think do wander round there thinking, 'Ah... the aphrodisiac of power,' which I have heard it described as, but I have never. It is not like that at all.

Judith Chalmers commented, 'You sound a bit disappointed in some ways?'

Marcia replied:

No, no, I have lived through it. I have seen it and the outside impression of it is glamorous just as the outside image of No. 10 is as a fantastically exciting and glamorous place to work. It is a place where a great deal of hard work is done. I worked long hours of hard work doing dreary boring stuff. That side of it you never see.

If I had the chance to rewind my life and do what I wanted to do, I doubt very much that I would have ended up in Downing Street, but I ended up there because Hugh Gaitskell died. If you put it back to the basic point, because but for that very tragic death Harold Wilson would not have become the leader of the Labour Party, and indeed not long before that death I had decided to read for the Bar – I thought I am not just interested in politics I am interested in the other side of justice and fairness – and I was on the point of doing it when Hugh died and the whole thing was changed and Harold said you will stay on and politics unfortunately became my life.

You hiccup through life. You hiccup from conference to election and stay on for the next election and you don't actually plot your life as you do in other professions. You have to play it by ear as you go along.

Judith asked if Marcia felt she had sacrificed her personal life?

'No, I wouldn't go as far as that. I take life as it comes. I think whatever happens is meant to be. I am very fatalistic. I think if that's how it's going to be, that's how it's going to be. I am very fatalistic about things.'

But why did Marcia have so much trouble with the press, asked Judith.

Oh, I think because it was a Labour government and on the whole I don't want to press this because these are the facts of life with which you have to live and you must to learn to deal with it, but I think the press and the media are on the whole more inclined towards the right of politics than on the left and therefore you suddenly get a Labour government that has been successful and in power for a long time and you get a lot of criticism and comment and then they go for the people not just at the centre but on the outskirts as well, and I was obviously one of the key targets for them. It was very unpleasant.

It wasn't because of what I did or what I said; it really was because I was a woman there and this I think is a very sad commentary on the lack of purpose there has been in British politics. It's true I think less even in the United States than it is here, where it has taken women a very long time to work their way to the top.

There have been outstanding women like the Prime Minister and Barbara Castle and Shirley Williams, but in the supportive roles it is much more difficult to get yourself to the top and it is very sad that we are like that and it is a loss, because a woman's view of everything and a woman's judgement and skills are very special and peculiar and it would be a good thing if we had more there, and I was the first one ever in that job and that's why there was a lot of attention focused on me. It wasn't like that for Douglas Hurd who is now at the Home Office, and nor was it for the guy who took over my job, Tom McNally who did the same job for Jim Callaghan.

If only I had been born Mark (instead of Marcia) Williams it would have been wonderful. So much easier.

Judith changed topic: 'You have two sons. They are not Mark, they are Tim and Dan and they are a very big part of your life.'

Marcia replied, 'They are a lovely part of my life and very special and I devote a great deal of my time to them.'

Judith then asked if Marcia was still continuing her working relationship with Harold?

Marcia said, 'Yes, I look after quite a bit of his work, not all of it but quite a bit of it still. I think that's right and I am happy to do it.'

Judith remarked that Harold was the longest-serving Prime Minister since the war, but Marcia added: 'So far yes, but I think that Mrs Thatcher will beat that record. He was there almost eight years. In January 1987, she will have beaten that.'

And, of course, Marcia with her impeccable political nous was right – Margaret Thatcher went on until 1990 before her colleagues forced her out.

Thames duly broadcast the interview in a daytime slot in 1984. It told the audience quite a lot about Marcia Falkender, but it didn't produce a rush of benefactors eager to save Marcia from the cruel treatment and appalling misjudgements she had suffered as the lone woman in the top team in 10 Downing Street.

20

Carrying-On in the Twenty-First Century

Marcia by the early twenty-first century had become an ill and unhappy woman. In 1998, she had had a brain aneurysm followed by a couple of strokes. She had spent more than a year in a private hospital being rehabilitated. The aneurysm had been on her right-hand side which was permanently damaged. For the rest of her life, she walked with a stick and she had to teach herself to write with her left hand. She was living back in Northamptonshire with her brother Tony and his wife Margarete and travelling to the House of Lords and back each working day by taxi. Marcia was still working with Harold and Mary, going regularly to their flat in Ashley Gardens when she was in town. Tony's health was declining and although Margarete believed he had done all he could to help Harold and support Marcia, he had been the loser. 'He got bugger all, just a stab in the back,' Margarete told me. She believes her whole family were damaged by their exposure as close friends and helpers to the family of Harold Wilson.

Up until the day Harold Wilson announced his shock resignation as Prime Minister, Marcia's troubles had remained largely a Westminster story. Yes, the political press all knew who she was and the incredible revelations about her young sons and her involvement as a shareholder in Tony Field's slag-gathering and land sales business in Ince-in-Makerfield could certainly have earned her a place in the Australian celebrity jungle in the twenty-first century in an attempt to redeem her reputation, but the general public knew little about her. She was somebody's sister and certainly somebody's secretary. All that ended with Harold's resignation honours list – the Lavender List thrust Marcia into the public spotlight as some kind of mysterious mastermind, controlling the Prime Minister behind the scenes. Dictating while pretending to take dictation who should be given honours at the end of Harold's premiership.

The Lavender List scandal made a scorching public reappearance in 2003 when Joe Haines brought out a new book, *Glimmers of Twilight*. The following year Bernard Donoughue published his autobiography *The Heat of the Kitchen*, followed in 2005 by his *Downing Street Diaries* which he had written at the end of every Downing Street day, carefully transcribing many of Marcia's tantrums and documenting her drug taking.

All three books got a great deal of attention, and a BBC producer put forward the idea of a drama documentary about the affair, *The Lavender List*.

The BBC liked the idea and hired Francis Wheen, the deputy editor of *Private Eye*, to write the script.

Wheen, like everybody at *Private Eye*, had followed the life of Marcia closely. To some extent she was *Private Eye*'s creature. Her name had morphed from Falkender to Forkbender in honour of Uri Geller who claimed an ability to bend cutlery. *Private Eye* had name-checked Marcia's boyfriends and babies many years before the mainstream press had the courage to go anywhere near the story. In the wake of her peerage, *Private Eye* had given her a cover spot and a new title: 'Lady Slagheap'.

Francis Wheen was excited about the project:

Almost the first thing I asked the producer, Alison Willett, was: have you been in touch with Marcia? She said they were leaving that until the thing was in production. Then she went to have tea with Marcia at the House of Lords (I think) and showed her a photo of Gina McKee, who was to play her in the film. Alison hoped Marcia would feel flattered to have such a wonderful actress in the role, but apparently not.

Wheen said the script went through various drafts, and each was scrutinised line by line by the BBC lawyers. He provided them with evidence to back up everything (including but not limited to the Haines and Donoughue accounts), and they gave it the all-clear.

When a letter arrived from the lawyers Carter-Ruck just days after transmission, the legal department were supremely unworried, especially since Marcia's main complaint was the allegation that the programme said she had a hand in Wilson's resignation honours list.

This idea was first speculated as long ago as 1977 in Joe Haines's *The Politics of Power* (over which she never sued) and repeated subsequently in countless Wilson biographies and histories of the 1970s (none of which she sued over). With Joe prepared to testify that his account was true, the lawyers didn't think she could possibly win if she actually sued. But over the following weeks, the BBC suddenly stopped answering Wheen's emails and phone messages when he tried to find out if she'd been seen off.

Suddenly, one day in April 2007, he was rung by a *Daily Telegraph* reporter, Neil Tweedie, with the news that the BBC was settling with Marcia – damages of £75,000, an apology and a promise that the film would never be shown again.

Incredulous, Wheen rang an executive in BBC drama. He explained that it was because the BBC had had to shell out £1 million or so to an Arab banker who had been wrongly accused (on the main evening TV news) of being al-Qaeda's money-launderer. An internal edict had come from on high that henceforth the corporation would instantly settle at the first whiff of a libel threat, regardless of the merits: no libel actions would be contested for the foreseeable future.

Wheen said:

> I put out a statement making it clear that I was not a party to the apology or settlement and was standing by the allegations in the film. Marcia was free to sue me, but of course she didn't. She would never have dared let a case like that actually get to court, where she could have been cross-examined.

Joe Haines had also believed that Marcia could never have handled a cross examination. Joe Stone, Harold Wilson's doctor, believed it too. That's why he continued to prescribe tranquillisers.

When Judith Chalmers asked Marcia why she had never spoken in her quarter of a century in the House of Lords, she replied confidently enough: 'I know the moment I do I shall be hooked on it. My own view of politics is that it is almost like a junkie and drugs or alcohol – you get hooked on it. They all get hooked on it.'

Videos of *The Lavender List* are occasionally posted on YouTube – but then swiftly taken down as soon as the BBC lawyers notice. Wheen told me:

I never met Marcia. I'm surprised to hear from you that she died in penury. How very odd. I'd have thought her regular libel threats/ settlements plus her rich benefactors would have been enough to keep her in funds. I know that Gerald Kaufman regularly went to visit her in her later years. And Illtyd Harrington, perhaps? Not sure who else kept in touch. Almost all her supporters and bene- factors – John Vaizey, Jimmy Goldsmith etc. – are now dead. How ironic that only her enemies – Haines and Donoughue – survive.

Joe Haines wrote *Glimmers of Twilight*, in which he portrayed Marcia as dangerous and difficult and responsible for the destruc- tion of Harold Wilson's legacy, twenty-seven years after Harold Wilson left office. Joe had joined Mirror Group Newspapers when he left Downing Street and was working there as a journalist when Robert Maxwell became the proprietor in 1984. Joe, always quick to judgement, announced immediately that the new proprietor was a crook and a liar and he could prove it. He expected to be sacked, but Robert Maxwell, who wanted to get Joe on side immediately, offered him the role of political editor of the Mirror Group. And it's fair to say Joe mellowed immediately. He then set out to write a rapid book about his boss designed to come out at around the same time as an unauthorised biography by Tom Bower. Bower's more-measured book garnered praise; Joe Haines's contribution was seen as a hagiography and not taken too seriously.

Having read everything Joe Haines had written about Marcia and initially put it all down to his puritanism and the fact that, at the time, Marcia was a woman in a man's world, I began to think I should go back and see Joe again. Maybe, if I did something no one had ever done for Marcia and put her case fairly to him, Joe might begin to see Marcia in a different light?

On 28 April 2023, I went to visit Joe Haines at his home in Tunbridge Wells. Just turned ninety-five, he looked frail but he was still absolutely on the button and keen to talk some more about his time with Harold and Marcia.

I had first visited Joe at home on 2 June 2021 to interview him about Marcia. He and his wife Irene were together in their living room. Irene listened carefully to what Joe had to say and when the interview was over, I asked her what she had thought of her husband's co-worker and she grimaced and said Marcia was a very wicked woman who had given Joe a great deal of misery. Quite often he would come home in the evening raging about how badly Marcia had behaved and how difficult she made life in No. 10.

The world had changed greatly since my last visit.

Irene died in September 2022. My own husband Austin Mitchell, who knew Joe very well indeed and had been personally accused by Joe of pelting Marcia with marshmallows after his sympathetic interview with her back in the 1970s, had also died, just a couple of months after my first visit to Joe and Irene. It had taken me quite a while to get moving on the story of Marcia again.

Marcia's story is dominated by the journalism of Joe and Bernard Donoughue, who joined No. 10 just before the first 1974 election. Throughout his time there, Bernard wrote a nightly diary which wasn't published until the twenty-first century, after Joe's *Glimmers of Twilight: Harold Wilson in Decline*, which Joe justifies on the grounds that thirty years before he had not been able to tell the complete inside story of Harold and Marcia.

I remarked to Joe that a lot of water has passed under the bridge in both our lives.

And Joe asked me how I was getting on with the book.

I explained that I had almost finished it, but I wanted to talk to him again to see if he could explain to me why he had waited nearly thirty years after Harold's departure from Downing Street and then seemingly set out again to attack Marcia.

Joe amazed me by suggesting that perhaps he hadn't been clear enough the first time we met what trouble had been caused by Marcia's whole family becoming involved with Harold.

I wondered if I had made it clear enough what a grip I think the Field family had on Harold. And I mean the Field *family*. Once Harold's book was published, Marcia got the *Sunday Times* to pay her sister Peg's salary for a year while she typed out Harold's manuscript and she moved her brother Tony, who is a whole book in himself, into the office as manager and the idea was to put my nose out of joint or possibly my whole body out of the organisation. So when we went to Northern Ireland in '72 I think it was, we were talking to everybody including Ian Paisley and the SDLP and we were staying at the Governor's House and I found that Tony Field had arranged that he and Harold would stay at the Governor's House and I would stay in a hotel in Lisburn, where a couple of weeks earlier in the town two British soldiers had been killed. I made it quite clear that I would not put up with that, I would stay in the Governor's House, or I would get the next plane back to London. That was just typical of Tony. He developed a crush on one of the girls in the office, it was an obsession. She used to do occasional secretarial work for me and I remember one evening in particular the door of my room burst open and Tony is standing there expecting to find me in a clinch with this girl. He didn't, he found I was dictating to her. Well, when Marcia discovered the depth of his obsession, she sacked the girl and then he developed a crush on Joe Kagan's secretary. When Marcia discovered that she brought the girl back into her office in the hope that her presence would distract Tony from Joe Kagan's secretary. It didn't work.

Joe then went back to talking again about Tony's wedding and how difficult that was for the Wilsons.

You know all about the wedding, and what happened and how [Marcia] pinched the Wilsons' plane and ended up at London Airport coming out of the Commonwealth exit and as she didn't have a passport, they demanded some proof of who she was. She didn't have a passport because you don't usually bring one if you are travelling from Leeds. But Harold and Mary, having had their plane stolen from them, were on the train back to London and they couldn't be contacted. And when eventually they did get hold of Harold, he explained who she was and then telephoned me because one of his pet obsessions was that every employee at Heathrow was in the pay of the *Sunday Times* and therefore the *Sunday Times* were going to get this story and when they got it, I was to delay them and give him a ring while we put together a story trying to explain this. But nothing happened, and she still kept her brother on as office manager. She tried to put her family in charge of No. 10.

I pointed out to Joe that when he first arrived at No. 10 in the late '6os, he had been quite impressed with Marcia.

Yes, I didn't know her well. She seemed to be pleasant and efficient, and when I first got to know her and I went to No. 10 and I got to work with her, I thought she had a very sharp political brain – better than any woman I had met. I was very impressed with her and she was very keen to involve me in everything.

Although I was a civil servant, I was involved on the political side from the beginning with Marcia and that carried on over the general election, when I wrote the first one or two speeches I wrote for Harold, until the leaving party incident, which turned everything upside down. You remember that. This was crucial to me. We went into opposition and Marcia had an office of nine secretaries which was absurd. Harold came out of No. 10 with a £14,000 overdraft, so he didn't have the money to pay them. Transport House were only paying him £6,000. Marcia treated the secretaries with some contempt and there was one girl from Bromley, independent, high spirited and she was not going to put up with Marcia. She resigned and on the afternoon she was leaving, she had a small party for the girls, you know, tea and cake, and she invited me because I got on well with them all. I went and thought nothing of it, but then when Harold and I were working on his book – he had written part of it and I had substantially rewritten the first chapter so that you would not have recognised it, but I made it much more readable. It's not boasting, I was a good journalist. We were working on it and suddenly the door opened. The doors always flew open, Marcia didn't knock and gently walk in, the door flew open and she demanded that Harold should sack me. I said, 'Why?' and she said, 'Because you are disloyal.' I said how was I disloyal and she revealed I had gone to this leaving party of the secretary who was leaving because she didn't like Marcia and I said, 'Well, yes, in that case I am guilty.' Harold tried to calm her down and she demanded if he didn't sack me, she was going and all that. Anyway, he got her out of the room eventually, but it had its consequences, you see, and she said, 'You are to have nothing whatsoever to do with this book.' Well, that doomed it from the start.

Of course I then asked Joe why he thought she did such things.

Because it was all about control, and the book was slipping out of her control. While Harold was writing the manuscript, Peg was typing the script and then I looked at it and I had rewritten it. It sounds complicated but with me I wrote very quickly in those days and I reckon I still could. Harold said, 'We are going to have to do something. I tell you what, I will write the book and I will let you see the proofs.' What she didn't know was that the printers were about 200 yards from where I lived then, in the north end of Tonbridge, so I just walked up and asked for the proofs and I used to work on them at home. I reckon I cut about 50,000 words out of the book, mainly speeches but still very dull, and I think the *Sunday Times* paid over the odds for it in those days. It was about £260,000, of which she got £60,000 or £70,000. That was the turning point. From that moment on, she was determined to get rid of me. I had affronted her, I was getting too close to Harold, I was taking over the book and she wasn't going to have it.

So I asked a key question. Who was the most important person, Harold or Marcia?

Joe said it depended on the subject:

When Marcia announced she was going to Dublin to see the IRA, Harold was firm and powerful. 'NO, YOU ARE NOT,' he said. 'DON'T YOU DARE.' But then again once she had gone out of the room he said, 'We've got to do something about it. You go to Dublin.' I said, 'No, I am known to too many people in Dublin. If I go to Dublin, I am bound to be recognised.' So then I met them in secret in Lambeth.

I was getting nervous. 'So maybe Harold and Marcia were a partnership trying to run the country? Maybe all the things you have accused her of, maybe he should have stopped them?'

I was scared asking these questions of Joe. His memory was so good, his accusations so clear, his scorn so palpable.

'Of course he should have stopped them.'

'So why didn't he?'

We are back to the eternal puzzle.

When she described him using the C-word [Joe claims Marcia called Harold a cunt in front of him], I would have had her out on her neck immediately.

When she called Mary to her house, the secretary calling her employer's wife to her house, and told her that she had slept with Harold half a dozen times, he should have thrown her out.

I asked Joe if he thought he was being a bit unreasonable. These days everything has changed and although Marcia might have been ahead of the game in being an equal partner with Harold, did Joe feel she must behave as a respectful secretary who should do her boss's bidding? I argued that they were much closer than that. That they shared power between them because Harold was prepared to listen to what Marcia had to say, however unfair people thought it might have been. The sort of to-ing and fro-ing that usually happens behind closed doors between business partners or husbands and wives.

Joe didn't waste a second:

But not on policy. On the running of the office, on the treatment of individuals, I mean she did some wicked things. I have said this over and over again. I had Albert Murray phone me one night in tears. He had just bought a new house. He had a heavy mortgage he needed his salary to pay and because of some apparent affront by somebody in the office, Marcia decided to pay no one their salaries. Albert was actually in tears and he was a tough little cockney type. I phoned Harold immediately and he said he didn't believe it, and I told him he had better, and I told him he was actually wrong and he said it must be a mistake and I said it is not a mistake, she has withheld everybody's salary as well. So Harold said, 'Tell Albert I shall send him a personal cheque,' and that is what he did. She was all powerful in the political office.

'And do you think it is wrong that she was all powerful in the political office?'

'Yes, I do,' said Joe firmly and coldly.

'Do you think anyone could get away with that sort of behaviour today?'

'I hope not. I don't know anybody like her. She was unique.'

I tried to press my point again: 'But Marcia was more than a secretary, wasn't she? She was a partner in crime, if you like?'

'And she was corrupt. You have to remember that she was corrupt and she got him to perform corrupt things.'

'So you are saying she was more powerful and influential than he was?'

Joe's response was instantaneous. 'It depends what you are talking about. Not in government policy. NO. She had very little to do with policy. In running the political office, she was all powerful and that spilled over.'

I took a deep breath. 'Is it because she was a woman?'

Don't make that mistake, Linda. I grew up in a family of women. My father died when I was two. I had two sisters and my mother. I was well disciplined and I never had a prejudice of any kind. I would have sacked her instantly man or woman, and she should have been.

'Do you think civil servants were misogynistic about her in the first place when she first arrived in Downing Street?'

Well, I don't know what it was like when she first arrived in Downing Street. In the private office where the civil servants, the personal secretaries, used to sit, I was talking to the one who held Harold's diary and Marcia came in and threw a piece of paper down on his desk. 'What do you think you are doing? Why do you put this in the Prime Minister's diary without consulting me? Take it out.' She treated him with utter contempt. I would not have taken that from anyone, man or woman, the way she treated him. If it had been a man, I would have knocked him down, which I have done on other occasions to other people.

I asked Joe why he had waited thirty years and then brought the whole story up again.

Joe said it was because he never told the full story the first time:

I thought she was a continuing scandal in British politics and she was all powerful in the political office.

And it didn't stop there. She wrote to the whips in the House of Lords and asked them to circulate a letter to Labour lords saying she was short of money and would they contribute to a fund for her.

'In your life she was unique, was she? You thought she was more than the secretary she should have been?'

Yes, she was. I was going to write a final book about the last days of Harold Wilson but now I cannot see to read or write.

I spent all those years in Parliament. When I first went to the Press Gallery and sat in my seat, down below me on the floor of the House was Winston Churchill, then the Prime Minister. I knew of many plots and I frustrated some plots. I knew a great deal. My experience in Parliament goes back so long, and I have lived so long. There was never anyone else like Marcia.

I was a good friend of her lover Walter Terry. She destroyed that family, destroyed it. I remember when I was asked about her, I said, 'She wants a husband and she doesn't care whose it is.' Mavis, Walter Terry's wife, was a good woman and Marcia destroyed them.

I asked Joe if he could think of any reason why Marcia might have behaved the way she did.

She took drugs. Again. I told you what Joe Stone told me. He would not allow her to go in the witness box until he filled her up with drugs beforehand because he couldn't trust her. Joe Stone hated the woman, but he treated her because she was important to Harold.

In all my experience, and I have known a great many people in the Labour and the Conservative Parties and I know of a great many alleged scandals, I never met anyone like Marcia. I never met a woman with her sort of language and using it to the Prime Minister. I have got some regard for the institutions of this country, to call the Prime Minister what she called him, it is intolerable and I don't believe there has ever been another woman like her.

Now along with that she did have an acute political mind and she could get to the heart of a problem, but that deteriorated into just writing 'RUBBISH' in big letters over whatever Harold was proposing to say. But she was constantly conspiring to increase her control. She did everything she could to get rid of me. On the other hand, I had an upbringing which was a bit tougher than hers.

'So, after Harold resigned, did you follow her progress after that?'

She continued to make money. She got money from Goldsmith. She continued to ask for money. Even the House of Lords. She persuaded the House of Lords to pay her taxi fare into the House and back to Blisworth in Northamptonshire every day.

She wrote to Mrs Thatcher when Jim Callaghan was Prime Minister and there was a general election, offering her help in beating Callaghan. He had been her employer briefly before she joined Wilson.

I asked Joe if he believed she was clear-headed when she did that.

'I don't know what clear-headed means in the circumstances,' he said:

I think she was a naturally wicked woman. Well, she had become a wicked woman. I don't think she always was. She had an acute mind to choose Harold Wilson as the coming man in the Labour Party. An acute political insight. She was determined and single minded. Especially about Harold Wilson.

The change came after we lost office. I think she probably felt that keenly.

She was wicked, and I am being precise. She was wicked. I don't recall her showing any generosity of spirit, and as time went on, she became worse and worse. It was always me, me, me and money, money, money.

Harold assured me she was getting the same salary as I was, so I came home and said to my wife, 'You are not looking after our money very well because Harold tells me Marcia is getting the same money as I do, yet she has got two houses in the West End, one in Buckinghamshire, a car in Buckinghamshire, four or five servants and she has got the use of the Prime Minister's car and we have got only one house.' Of course Harold was lying.

I heard her treat Joe Kagan with utter contempt the day after we lost the 1970 general election. Well, I didn't like Kagan, so I thought she was just a woman in a bad temper but what I saw afterwards: the leaving party incident, the determination to get rid of me. The one thing she couldn't do was get rid of me. Nor could she get rid of my friends. She tried to get rid of Bernard Donoughue. She definitely made a play for him, and Harold Wilson phoned Bernard one night and said, 'She is off her head. She says she is going to phone the Press Association. She says she is going to spill the beans. Will you go round to her place and pull her telephone out of the wall?'

Later Marcia walked into Bernard's room and put a piece of paper on his desk saying, 'Hell hath no fury.'

I moved the conversation forward to Harold Wilson's resignation honours and asked Joe if he had tried to protest to Harold about Marcia's involvement in choosing the recipients.

He knew what my attitude was. I went to him and complained that one of those on the list was a Soviet agent, another was being investigated by the police, and he denied both of them. He must have known they were true.

I wouldn't blow the whistle. I was very fond of Harold, and I wasn't going to walk out and denounce him, but he knew jolly well that if he tried to sack me, I could blow him out of the water.

I wouldn't have actually. He did everything he could to avoid sacking me.

Nothing, nothing, not since the days of Lloyd George has there been such blatant sale of honours. And not since the days of Lloyd George have there been such people honoured such as Rudy Sternberg and others.

So the time had come to ask Joe for his final assessment of Marcia's contribution.

Did he think Marcia's influence over Harold diminished him as a Prime Minister?

I think it did him enormous damage to him as a Prime Minister. He had many good things going for him. I think the Open University counted for a lot. I think he had a genuine concern for people. He wasn't cynical. He was never rude. I never heard him say a rude world to a civil servant. He did the job but always there was this cloud.

And that cloud was called Marcia. On one occasion I said to him, 'Why don't you get rid of her?' He said, 'I have suspended her from coming into the office for six weeks'. I said, 'Harold, she doesn't come into the office!'

Joe continued:

I never met anyone else who approached her on a scale of evil, and I believe in evil.

She wrecked everybody. Her sister Peg, who was a nice girl and attractive in a strong way, physically more attractive than Marcia, she met a man in the park and they got friendly and they were going out. He told her he was a doctor and it was getting serious and she told Marcia about him. Marcia demanded of Harold that he get the Flying Squad to investigate the man. The police investigated him, and he turned out to be a porter at the hospital. And that was the end of that romance.

I pointed out that Marcia had done Peg a great favour in exposing the truth.

'You could say that, but it was none of her business. But then you have to consider how she tried to wreck Tony's marriage to Margarete by bringing this secretary back who she sacked because she thought that the secretary was too close to Tony.'

I explained to Joe that it was my belief that Marcia should get enormous credit for what she had done to promote and advise Harold and manage the political side of the 1960s and '70s Labour governments. Surely she had earned a special place in British history for what she had done for the Labour Party?

To my amazement, Joe agreed. 'I think she should have a special place. She was unique.'

I also pointed out that many Labour people regretted the fact that they had never had a female leader.

Joe's tone changed immediately:

That's a different thing altogether. She would never have been a leader. She was totally incapable of making public speeches. Totally. She never made one in the House of Lords.

She had to go there because she ran out of money. She was getting £300 a day each time she went to the Lords.

And then he turned back to the honours again. 'In those days, I took a serious view about honours. When I saw Harold had got David Frost down for a peerage, I said to him he would bring the list into disrepute and he shouldn't do it.'

I asked if this was because of Frost's relationship with Trident, the owners of both Tyne Tees and Yorkshire Television.

'No!' he said with exasperation. 'Just because he was a television entertainer, that's all. I knew Frost a lot better than Harold did.'

But if we can give honours to cricketers and tennis players, why can't we give them to television people? I was puzzled.

At last Joe admitted that we were talking about different days.

'So, you do think the situation has changed somewhat?'

He replied:

Deteriorated. Anyone can get them now. Today you could give David Frost a peerage and nobody would mind. In those days, people would have minded and I would have minded and I told Harold. I had a free and easy relationship with Harold; I could tell him anything.

Then one day he said to me I am down to have dinner tonight with David Frost and Jimmy Goldsmith and I don't even know him. So, he cancelled it and of course Marcia reinstated it, so Harold had dinner with Goldsmith. Next day I said how did it go? He said OK, he had quite an interesting knowledge of the French planning system. That's all he said. So he made Goldsmith a knight. It was never intended to make him a peer, but she got money from Goldsmith. Marcia got money from Goldsmith; he paid the boys school fees. That's why she had that sort of influence.

I remembered what Richard Ingrams had said about Marcia and Goldsmith and their joint determination to defeat *Private Eye*, but I didn't mention it to Joe again. Nothing was going to change his view of Marcia and the power he believed she wielded over Harold Wilson and his Labour governments.

Suddenly, without me saying any more, Joe went back to Marcia:

> She had this obsession with show business. When we had dinner at No. 10, I remember looking at the seat placements and she was down on one wing of the horseshoe. She picks it up and moves her place so she was sitting next to Paul Scofield, and somebody who was sitting next to Scofield ended up in her place. And why should Harold honour the Delfont brothers? She liked being in the circle, she brought them all into No. 10.

And there we were back at the beginning of Marcia's story. Marcia the teenager at Northampton High School with her friend Ann Cauldwell, both of them passionate movie-goers. Both of them writing letters to all the American film stars they saw at their local cinema, ever hopeful that they would get replies that they could add to their autograph books. In everyone's life some passions last from beginning to end, and that's how it was with Marcia.

Conclusion

The Importance of Marcia

When Marcia Falkender died in 2019, Julia Langdon, *The Guardian*'s brilliant obituarist, wrote:

> It was a matter of universal agreement during the years of Harold Wilson's leadership of the Labour Party that his private and political secretary, Marcia Williams, who has died aged 86, was the single most influential figure among his staff. She exerted an unrivalled degree of power throughout his four periods in office as Prime Minister and ran his office for 27 years, but became a source of conflict and division that clouded his years in Downing Street and ultimately diminished his political standing.

It was fair and just. But not the sort of thing that most of Marcia's contemporaries of both sexes would have gone along with. When rare women got to the top in the 1960s and '70s, there usually had to be a clear explanation for their triumph.

For the rest of us, just as equality had begun to be talked about as an exciting possibility, a protest against a Miss America beauty pageant in New Jersey sparked the mythical and soon to be iconic image of the 'bra-burning feminist'.

A group of women hurled floor-mops, lipsticks and high-heeled shoes into a 'Freedom Trash Can'.

The idea was to symbolically throw away things that oppressed women, said Robin Morgan, one of the organisers. Passers-by were invited to join in. 'I remember one young woman took off her bra, eased it out from under her shirt and threw it in to great cheers.'

It was a gesture that made headlines around the world, securing the protesters a place in history.

In 1968, I was twenty-seven and the mother of year-old twins. I had arrived in the UK from New Zealand, where I had met Austin Mitchell because we had been chance paired as a presenter (him) and researcher (me) in newly begun NZ television (just thirty years behind the BBC). But Austin then accepted a post at Nuffield College, Oxford, in an attempt to kill off his newfound passion for TV. I stuck to mine and struggled through my first year as a young mum in the UK travelling by train to London and then by Tube to the BBC at Shepherd's Bush for four long days every week on 24 *Hours*, the then equivalent of *Newsnight*. I left home at 7 a.m. and got back at midnight. We had live-in childcare from the 'National Council for the Unmarried Mother and her Child', accompanied by her baby. We shared a triplet pushchair. I got the sack from the BBC at the end of my first year. 'Not that there was anything wrong with your work,' said my boss John Grist, head of the current affairs group, but with two small babies he claimed I didn't really have the time others had to devote to the programme. I am pleased to see that such discriminatory employment practices are much less common today.

By this time, stories of 'bra-burning feminists' had spread around the world and people used to tease me. They could hear that I was a feminist. I went on about it a bit. They kept asking, did I really go around burning my bras? I don't think I ever came up with a good answer.

Austin decided academia wasn't for him and took a job as a presenter at the brand-new Yorkshire Television in Leeds in 1969. I made do with a job at the BBC in Manchester, directing *Look North*. My commute became tougher. Bradford to Manchester five days a week. Out of the house twelve hours a day with a local live-in nanny to look after the twins. All I can say, looking back, was that I loved television too much. I knew I was good at it and I never seriously considered for even a minute giving it up. For the next fifty years, I battled and travelled, tried my best with the kids, tried even harder when Austin became an MP and I had to extend my endless commuting to a triangle which included London and Grimsby. Shirley Conran, author of *Superwoman*, said that women could do everything, and along with the spirit of the age, I gave it my best shot. Of course, Conran was wrong and so was I. Women could get on brilliantly if they found someone who shared some of the load, but so often so many of us were forced to follow Conran's mantra and fail.

I didn't give much thought to any of this until 2015 when Austin was coming up eighty. He had been an MP for thirty-seven years and decided to retire. He had not been well since 2010, when the brilliant Professor Ajay Shah at King's College Hospital had diagnosed heart failure but promised him another ten years if he had an operation and a rest. So we came home to Yorkshire to end our commuting for good. Austin got his promised ten years and a bit more and died in August 2021. Physically absorbed with my caring duties, I started thinking about my time in telly, our time in politics and how other women of my generation had managed.

I came across Marcia Williams because she was a friend of Austin's. He had always admired Harold Wilson, who had returned to the back benches in the Commons for the first six years of Austin's career as an MP, and of course I knew and liked the Kagan family, who lived close to us in Calderdale and were so central to Marcia's story.

I started researching the life of Marcia and delving into the wide-ranging supply of 1960s and '70s political books Austin had collected and was now intent on passing on to me. The first and most important was Ben Pimlott's *Harold Wilson*, a brilliant biography never bettered, and I now consider it to be even more distinguished because it gave Marcia such a fair appraisal. Pimlott gave Marcia full credit for what she had achieved politically; I could find no others as generous.

Writing about Marcia as the central character in this book turned out to be harder than I ever imagined possible.

Marcia herself was a very private person indeed, rarely giving interviews. Her last contact with the press before her death was a feature by Polly Dunbar which appeared in the *Mail on Sunday* in 2018. It was an exclusive interview with Marcia, where she set out to 'rescue her legacy and that of Wilson from years of smear and innuendo'. The article garnered attention because it published for the first time a photograph of the original Lavender List. It rehashed the old Joe Haines derision with contributions from others eager to blame Marcia for an unsatisfactory end to Harold Wilson's time as Prime Minister. There was a large accompanying photograph of Marcia looking as I had never seen her before. Gone was the elegant and poised blonde who was head of the political office in Downing Steet, replaced by an uncertain looking old lady in a button-up cardigan reminiscent of Queen Elizabeth's outfit for her last public engagement with Prime Minister Liz Truss.

Marcia's remaining family are also very private. Her parents and siblings are all gone but Marcia has two sons, Tim and Dan. Neither wished to speak publicly about Baroness Falkender.

The only family member I could talk to, and it was in infrequent conversations sometimes months apart, was Margarete Field, Tony Field's widow, Marcia's sister-in-law and Joe Kagan's secretary. Margarete still lives in the home near Northampton that she and Tony bought after their marriage. She didn't really want to talk to me in the beginning, but we had such a lot in common, both recent widows, me living just a few miles from her childhood home in Calderdale. Both of us trying and failing to sell large family homes and move away. Margarete is as bitter as Joe Haines in her descriptions of Marcia as cruel and mean. But she sees her as a cruel and mean sister to Tony, not the destroyer of a Prime Minister's reputation. Margarete believes, and I think she is probably right, that Tony was kind and compassionate to his sisters but got nothing in return. The saga of the Lavender List seemed very personal to Margarete. Where everyone else was complaining that Marcia had been responsible for spreading lashings of honours to undeserving recipients, Margarete kept telling me Tony got nothing. Bugger all. He had given his time generously to Harold without payment and tried to protect and support his sisters, but Marcia had made sure he got nothing.

I decided to look further afield and visit Marcia's old school in my search for information. Northampton High School seemed a splendid place. Really helpful and polite girls bouncing everywhere, eager to help a strange visitor. The alumnae officer put me in touch with Ann Cauldwell, Marcia's great friend in the sixth form at school, because she had written an obituary of Marcia for the school magazine in 2019, and to be honest I don't think they knew much else or had much interest in Marcia. The girls I spoke to had certainly never heard of her and there is no mention of her on the school website.

Northampton itself has got a rather proud record of distinguished female politicians. Margaret Bondfield, one of the first three female Labour MPs and the first female Cabinet minister, was MP for Northampton from 1923 to 1924, and Maureen Colquhoun, the MP for Northampton North from 1974 to 1979, was the first openly lesbian MP.

Even so, Northampton High School seemed an unlikely place to find a socialist leader growing up. Marcia explained it a bit herself in her interview with Judith Chalmers. Janet Margesson, daughter of a Tory Chief Whip, was her French teacher, and apparently she was only too keen to talk to the girls about her own passionately held left-wing views. Her father David Margesson was a very popular Chief Whip between the wars when there was a national government. He was considered tough but successful at getting people from at least three political parties to work together. Janet may well have excited Marcia's interest in left-wing politics, but there really was only one person in Marcia's life who brought together passion and politics: James Harold Wilson.

When she got her first job at Labour headquarters after graduating from university and completing a secretarial course, Marcia, who had a very junior post, understood immediately that Labour needed a much stronger relationship with voters across Britain than Gaitskell and his arty and intellectual colleagues could ever produce. Marcia watched Harold Wilson carefully as he moved around the country visiting local Labour Parties and trying to come up with a national structure that was fair to all and gave encouragement to workers that Labour would help them to move up in the world. She could see that her bosses were very much to the right of Harold Wilson and much less interested in equality of local parties in distant counties than Harold was. So she wrote to him anonymously and encouragingly several times to warn him about what was going on in head office long before they met in person. It was an incredibly smart and bold move from a young political novice. She appreciated and shared his passion for equality. As Marcia said to Judith Chalmers, Harold Wilson's genius was that he gave the working man a chance to get on.

Once they had met on that night of political magic, 23 April 1956, Harold and Marcia were never really apart again. Marcia's love for Harold was heady and believable. She spoke of how her hands trembled as she took shorthand notes of Khrushchev's contribution and Gaitskell's closing speech that night, and saw that Harold was watching her carefully. There was magic abroad in the air and angels dancing in the Ritz for many years to come.

George Caunt, who worked first in Labour head office and then closely with Harold and Marcia in the 1964 election, could see how intimate they were in their first years together. Looking at how Marcia behaved with other lovers throughout her life, it is easy to see that she was obsessed with Harold and wanted what passionately she believed they could achieve together. But it is also easy to understand that Harold would see things differently. Tightly knit together with Mary and their children, it is perfectly possible that he was a man with a plan almost from the beginning of his relationship with

Marcia. He almost certainly allowed sexual seduction by Marcia, but he probably quickly saw it as irrelevant to the main plan for his future in British politics.

Mary and the boys were always going to be an important part of his life but not the political part. So there was no reason why he and Marcia shouldn't go forward with a different kind of relationship, where she was the mistress of the political sphere, and Mary kept her relationship with Harold and her family at home, which was where she wanted to be. Harold was good at compartmentalisation. When he was working so hard for Sir William Beveridge at University College, he often gave up his weekends to travel with him to his home in Avebury in Wiltshire. Harold kept his working life rigorously divided from his life with Mary. She was never invited to go with him to Avebury.

So, after a romantic initial relationship, as observed by George Caunt, there is little doubt that Harold and Marcia settled down into a political partnership. He developed his ideas. She developed the machinery to make them work. She worked her fingers to the bone to get him elected as leader of the Labour Party and then as Prime Minister. It was a staggering feat by them both, and Marcia could see clearly just what her own role had been and how important she was to the future of the Labour Party, not so much as a government, for that was not her role, but more for the well-being of the party which supported that government. The Labour Party head office never understood and never gave enough credit to Marcia for what she did. They were stuck firmly in the 1950s with the old hierarchical structures. Men at the top. Men in charge. Women firmly in second place as housewives and homemakers and everything else they could cram into their busy days. Marcia was different. She understood clearly what 'party' meant and she knew where the support had to come from to keep the Labour Party in power.

Where she began to slip and slide was in the way she presented her case for help. She was frightened and angry that the party head office couldn't or wouldn't give Harold the support he needed for Marcia to run things successfully. There really was no money. There had been a tendency with the 1964 election to run things on two fronts. When she answered the phone, Marcia pretended to be a whole host of people supporting Harold; it was a successful ruse, but she couldn't go on like that once Labour were in power. Yes, the civil servants could take the lead role in running the country with the Prime Minister, but she strongly believed she had the right to another lead role running the party which supported the Prime Minister, and that's where it all started to go awry. Marcia was driving with a tireless passion and excitement. It was something that had never been seen in Downing Street before and it was too easy for people to look at her driven enthusiasm and misinterpret it as bossiness, even craziness. She knew what she wanted, and she demanded it forcefully.

But behind all that was a British woman who could also see what she was missing out on. She had accepted Harold's amazing skill at compartmentalising his life. He had demanded and got one life at home and another in the office. He enjoyed his steady relationship with Mary and the boys. The reliability of it all, the peace of it all. A blessing quite a lot of the time because it gave him a rest from the turbulence of the office. Marcia had nothing like that. No home life to speak of. We will never know what kind of relationship led to her marriage to Mr Williams, but it was quickly diagnosed by her as a massive mistake when she saw what Harold Wilson had to offer. There is no doubt at all that he was the love of her life.

It is true that she screamed and shouted. She was frightened, she panicked and she got out of control. But no one offered Marcia any help and support. No one looked beyond the tantrums to see that she was clearly in distress. Only Harold, who probably never listened very much anyway, having got used to her ranting, got on with his work.

So Marcia, for all her brilliant contributions to Harold Wilson becoming Prime Minister, became jumpy and nervous in her relations with her co-workers in Downing Street. She was overworked and she was underpaid, she had given up her marriage to take on Harold's future and although she was delighted with what she had achieved, she wanted more. She could see that Harold was happy at home with Mary and the boys. She thought he had an enviable home life.

And that was where the decline in Marcia's self-control began. She started by taking purple hearts so that she could manage long hours without sleep and she went on ruling the political roost in Downing Street, often shouty, often upset, keeping her own private life – her relationship with Walter Terry and the rapid arrival within ten months of each other of her sons – a carefully guarded secret.

When Bernard Donoughue arrived to work for Harold Wilson, he was amazed and somewhat enchanted by her.

I get the feeling that everything Harold does in politics is to please her. He does not care about the people, the party or himself. She is the daughter who he delights in, however outrageous, and who he is working to please. It is amazing to watch. His patience with her is endless.

But thanks to Dr Joseph Stone, the Prime Minister's medical adviser, Marcia was going to need much patience from everyone she worked and lived with for the rest of her life. Dr Stone like Joe Haines was a huge admirer of the Prime Minister. He thought he was doing a fantastic job for Britain, but he saw Marcia as a huge impediment to his progress. Haines and Stone both found Marcia's behaviour offensive. Both men saw the Prime Minister as the ultimate boss, and if Marcia shouted and told him what to do, she was draining his power away. They both believed that people unlucky enough to see them together would be shocked that the British Prime Minister could be shouted at and abused by a young secretary. Neither of them could understand Harold's relationship with Marcia. It worried them hugely, but they didn't know what to do about it. Joe Haines said he could never tolerate a person who swore like that at the Prime Minister, and Joe Stone thought it was deeply wrong that the Prime Minister should have to tolerate such abusive behaviour. Neither believed that Harold could handle Marcia. Both believed that they had to DO something.

Joe Stone started to prescribe Marcia large quantities of Valium, believing it would control her and calm her down. Those who watched her use it from a vial she wore on a chain around her neck said she sometimes took it by the handful. We cannot blame Stone for prescribing her Valium; the mistake he made was in common with every other GP in the land. It was some years before they began to realise how addictive benzodiazepines were and how hard it was to get people off them after long and heavy misuse. But it was no wonder that people described Marcia as having a mercurial temperament – she was under the influence of not only the purple hearts but the prescribed Valium – and no one was there to support her.

In the end, Joe Stone did go too far. Joe Haines reports that Stone suggested to him and Bernard Donoughue that they 'dispose' of Marcia (put her down, kill her) in the interest of freeing Harold from the burden he believed she had become.

Of course they were shocked and rejected his suggestion outright. It certainly wouldn't have worked. No one has ever been asked to imagine what sort of Prime Minister Harold Wilson would have been without Marcia Falkender to guide and advise him. It's almost impossible to imagine.

The story of Marcia is an incredibly sad one. No one ever wondered if she was ill, if she needed help to escape from the dreadful addiction which was dragging her down. No one, not even Harold. Most people who worked with her asked the same old question, what hold did she have over Harold that encouraged her to believe she could get away with such behaviour? Of course it was the wrong question. Marcia saw herself as protecting Harold and herself from the unreasonable demands of others who failed to understand the situation they were in, trying to run the country.

Marcia lived at a time, only a few decades ago, when women's role in society was firmly cemented in place as unequal to that of men. When a woman like Marcia came along who had something new to offer, she could be listened to only if she played men's games to men's rules. If 'her voice was ever soft, gentle and low, an excellent thing in a woman'.

A very great deal has changed in sixty years. Keir Starmer, determined to get the best help available should he become Prime

Minister, has been very keen to secure the services of Wonder Woman Sue Gray to run his office. Everyone understands today the value of a great organiser to control the political mayhem that surrounds a new Labour government and its leader.

Attitudes towards single and unmarried parents have also improved greatly since Marcia's time. For over five years, she did everything she could to cover up the birth of her sons Tim and Dan. Like fewer than 5 per cent of births in 1968, they were illegitimate. Today the majority of babies born in the UK are the children of parents who are not married to each other.

There is nothing we can do now to change the circumstances which affected Marcia's life so desperately. Those of us who lived through the 1960s and '70s have seen the great changes which swept away the rules sent down from the Establishment perched at the top of the tree.

When Harold Wilson's premiership was over, Marcia continued her career as a politician in the House of Lords. She lived long enough to be the longest-serving Labour peer, but she never made a speech in the Lords. Many said she attended daily just to collect the attendance allowance. When she was ill and fragile in the first decades of the new century, she wrote to the Lords whips asking that they should suggest to members that she was old and poor and needed help with her bills. Some were sympathetic and kind but embarrassed to talk about the help they gave. Others were appalled that a woman who they believed had been a harridan and a seller of peerages should go begging from their lordships.

Marcia Falkender's ashes have been tucked in unmarked in a plot with her parents in the graveyard at All Saints' Church in West Haddon, Northamptonshire.

Hers was an incredibly romantic story. The young autograph-hunter who loved the movies and wrote to American film stars hoping for a letter by return, transformed into a Prime Minister's right-hand woman.

When she went to work in Labour's head office in the 1950s, Marcia picked a winner, a star. She encouraged, guided and promoted him. She made it possible for Harold Wilson to win a still unmatched four general elections for the Labour Party. Marcia was incredibly proud of what Harold had achieved. It was as if she was recreating, just for him, the memory of his mother Ethel bursting with pride when her brainy Yorkshire lad made it to Oxford university.

But Marcia, the brilliant politician, the A1 organiser, the tireless campaigner, paid a heavy price. The world wasn't yet ready to extend a helping hand to the woman who had pushed Harold Wilson to the top. It is time Marcia receives the respect she has long deserved, for being a trailblazer and the first woman to wield real power in Downing Street.

Bibliography

Books

Arnold, Catharine, *Edward VII*, St Martin's Press, 2017

Aronson, Theo, *The King in Love: Edward VII's Mistresses*, Thistle Publishing, 2014

Castle, Barbara, *The Castle Diaries, 1974–76*, Weidenfeld & Nicolson, 1980

Cole, John, *As It Seemed to Me: Political Memoirs*, Weidenfeld & Nicolson, 1991

Donoughue, Bernard, *Downing Street Diary: With Harold Wilson in No. 10*, Jonathan Cape, 2005

— —, *The Heat of the Kitchen: An Autobiography*, Politico's, 2004

Dorril, Stephen and Robin Ramsay, *Smear! Wilson and the Secret State*, Fourth Estate, 1991

Falkender, Marcia, *Downing Street in Perspective*, Weidenfeld & Nicolson, 1983

— —, *Inside Number 10*, Weidenfeld & Nicolson, 1972

Foot, Paul, *The Politics of Harold Wilson*, Penguin, 1968

Haines, Joe, *Glimmers of Twilight: Harold Wilson in Decline*, Politico's, 2003

— —, *Kick 'em Back: Wilson, Maxwell and Me*, Grosvenor House, 2019

— —, *The Politics of Power*, Jonathan Cape, 1977

Lapping, Brian, *The Labour Government, 1964–70*, Penguin, 1970

Leigh, David, *The Wilson Plot: The Intelligence Services and the Discrediting of a Prime Minister*, Pantheon Books, 1988

Mitchell, Austin and David Wienir, *Last Time: Labour's Lessons from the Sixties*, Bellew, 1997

Morgan, Austen, *Harold Wilson: A Life*, Pluto Press, 1992

Morgan, Janet ed., *The Backbench Diaries of Richard Crossman*, Hamish Hamilton, 1981

Pimlott, Ben, *Harold Wilson*, HarperCollins, 1992

Richards, Steve, *The Prime Ministers: Reflections on Leadership from Wilson to May*, Atlantic Books, 2019

Roth, Andrew, *Sir Harold Wilson: Yorkshire Walter Mitty*, MacDonald and Jane's, 1977

Sandbrook, Dominic, *State of Emergency: Britain, 1970–74*, Allen Lane, 2010

Thomas-Symonds, Nick, *Harold Wilson: The Winner*, Weidenfeld & Nicolson, 2022

Wigg, George, *George Wigg by Lord Wigg*, Michael Joseph, 1972

Wilson, Harold, *The Governance of Britain*, Weidenfeld & Nicolson and Michael Joseph, 1976

— —, *The Labour Government, 1964–1970: A Personal Record*, Weidenfeld & Nicolson, 1971

— —, *Memoirs: The Making of a Prime Minister, 1916–1964*, Weidenfeld & Nicolson and Michael Joseph, 1986

Other Sources

Bodleian Library, Oxford, the papers of Harold Wilson

British Library

Queen Mary, University of London Archives: Queen Mary College; QMC/CUB/2; CUB, 14 May 1954

Thames Television, interview with Marcia Falkender by Judith Chalmers, FremantleMedia UK, 1984

University of Hull Library, the papers of Austin Mitchell

Acknowledgements

It hasn't been easy for me, writing about Marcia. I never met her, but I have come to admire her for all the good things she did for the Labour Party, for women and for politics in general.

Britain now has little memory of those who have gone before. They live on only in the hearts of those who loved them. I am no historian, but I am a storyteller, and the tale of Marcia and Harold is one that every young person, striving to make the world a better place, deserves to know.

There is no doubt that Marcia was a brilliant politician, tactician and organiser. Without her, there's a fair chance Labour might have failed to make it into power in 1964. That would have been a great loss.

I have made many new friends in my search for Marcia. Ann Burrows (née Cauldwell), Marcia's dear friend in the sixth form at Northampton High School, has been my adviser and guide to all things Marcia for two years now.

Margarete Field, widow of Tony Field and Marcia's sister-in-law, told me the story of her family and her working life as Joe Kagan's secretary. She was brave and truthful.

Pauline Windross enchanted me with the tales of her trips to London to greet Marcia's newborn babies and give them a flying start.

Jenny Kagan, who was a sparky little girl when I knew her last, is now a feisty adult from the marvellous Kagan family remembered so warmly in West Yorkshire.

Professor Jon Davis, director of the Strand Group at King's College London, was kind and patient with my amateur attempts to understand the role of the civil service in No. 10.

Mary Aylmer, Ian Hislop, Francis Wheen and everyone at *Private Eye* were helpful in every way. *Private Eye* has been part of my life for sixty years now; telling stories of the 1960s and '70s would be impossible without their kindness, their input and their brilliant filing system.

Lord Butler of Brockwell told me the incredible story of how Marcia tried to get him sacked, and of course the two main players from 10 Downing Street, Joe Haines and Bernard Donoughue, talked to me a great deal about Marcia. Thanks to them all.

Everyone at my publisher, Biteback – my brilliant editor Ella Boardman, Suzanne Sangster, James Stephens and Olivia Beattie – were all essential to the success of this project.

My dear legal friend Ian Bloom and my football consultant Jackie Hay in New Zealand helped and supported me when dark clouds loomed.

Finally, I have been boring the whole of my much-loved Mitchell family with tales of Marcia and Westminster in the 1960s and '70s for two years now, and at last I shall stop.

Linda McDougall
Sowerby Bridge
West Yorkshire
September 2023

Index